CORRIDORS
THROUGH
TIME

A HISTORY OF
THE VICTORIA FALLS HOTEL

About the Author

Peter Roberts is a researcher and writer on the natural and human history of the Victoria Falls. Born in Wales and an ecologist by training, Peter has become drawn to the landscapes, wildlife and human history of Africa and especially the natural wonder of the Falls and its surrounds. Following the success of his first book, 'Sun, Steel and Spray - a History of the Victoria Falls Bridge,' published in 2011, Peter now presents this detailed, informative and entertaining history of the Victoria Falls Hotel.

Also Available

To the Banks of the Zambezi and Beyond -
Railway Construction from the Cape to the Congo (1893-1910).
Life and Death at the Old Drift, Victoria Falls (1898-1905).
Sun, Steel and Spray - A History of the Victoria Falls Bridge.
Footsteps Through Time - A History of Travel and Tourism to the Victoria Falls.

- - -

Corridors Through Time - A History of the Victoria Falls Hotel
Peter Roberts

Copyright © 2021 Peter Roberts. All Rights Reserved
www.zambezibookcompany.com

First Published September 2015, Jafuta Foundation
Second Edition July 2016, Zambezi Book Company
Third Edition April 2021, Zambezi Book Company

Cover design and page layout by Peter Roberts

ISBN: 9798728675723

Roberts, Peter (2021) Corridors Through Time - A History of the Victoria Falls Hotel Third Edition, Zambezi Book Company / CreateSpace Independent Publishing

CORRIDORS THROUGH TIME

A HISTORY OF THE VICTORIA FALLS HOTEL

PETER ROBERTS

Contents

Early view of the first Victoria Falls Hotel buildings

Foreword
A Grand Old Lady

It is a pleasure to introduce Peter's second book, 'Corridors Through Time,' covering the rich history of The Victoria Falls Hotel and its central role in the development of travel and tourism to the Victoria Falls.

It has been my privilege to have had a close working relationship with this most magnificent of hotels for almost two decades, including the honour of being its General Manager from 2009-2011, guiding the Hotel through perhaps of the most difficult periods of operation in its history.

I have a particular fondness for the Hotel, for it is also where I met my wife, Nicole, during my first period working at the Hotel, as Deputy General Manager, in 1999. Ten years later, with Nicole's valuable assistance and the support of a dedicated staff team, we guided the Hotel through some of her most challenging days.

Over the long period of its operation the Hotel has taken on an identity of her own, 'The Grand Old Lady of the Falls,' matriarch of Zimbabwe's tourism industry. She has had her ups, and downs, but from modest beginnings she has matured into a global icon, ranked among the most famous hotels of the world.

The Hotel is not only dedicated to meeting the needs of tourists, but is also the heart of the community of Victoria Falls, which has grown up around the Hotel and Railway Station. The Hotel has provided employment for many, business opportunities for some, but most importantly a place of rest and relaxation for all.

On behalf of those, like myself, who have been intimately involved in the fortunes of the Hotel, I congratulate Peter on his detailed history. 'Corridors Through Time' is more than the history of a Hotel - it is the story of the development of modern tourism to the Victoria Falls through the twentieth century.

Karl Snater
General Manager
The Victoria Falls Hotel (2009-2011)

Preface

Welcome to this history of The Victoria Falls Hotel, 'Grand Old Lady of the Falls,' and a journey through over a century of travel and tourism to the Victoria Falls. In presenting this history, I have, wherever possible, described events directly through contemporary references and descriptions, quotations from which form a key element of the text. Many references have been used to compile this work, and I have referenced as much material as possible as these sources will be of interest to those wishing to know more about the history of this fascinating Hotel.

The names of places and countries have changed over the years, and old names are first introduced in their original historical contexts, whilst also identified with their contemporary names for clarity, for example Rhodesia (now Zimbabwe). It should be noted that for ease of reading the text often refers to the 'Railway Company', rather than the full operating company title of the Beira and Mashonaland and Rhodesia Railways, changed to simply Rhodesia Railways in 1927 and becoming Rhodesia Railways, Limited, in 1936. Following nationalisation the company became a statutory body, the Rhodesia Railways, in 1949, and finally renamed the National Railways of Zimbabwe in 1980.

I have tried to avoid repeated references to ever increasing monetary amounts, for example room rates and tourist tariffs. However, reference is occasionally made to significant sums at their contemporary value, historically in Rhodesian pounds (originally pegged to the British pound), before being replaced by the Rhodesian dollar in 1970, and later Zimbabwe dollar in 1980 and finally the adopted US dollar.

I apologise for any errors, mistakes or omissions in the text, which I hope are few in number and small in nature. Comments and criticisms are welcomed, as are contributions; especially information or stories missing from this account. Additional information, amendments, updates and notification of future revised editions will be published online at www.zambezibookcompany.com. Readers interested in the wider history of the development of tourism to the Victoria Falls during the twentieth century will also be interested in the companion publication 'Footsteps Through Time - A History of Travel and Tourism to the Victoria Falls' (Roberts, 2021b).

I hope you enjoy reading the story of this icon of the Falls and exploration of its central role in the development of tourism at this most notable of natural wonders.

Peter Roberts
April 2021
peter@zambezibookcompany.com

Introduction

Associated by some as a symbol of colonial ambition and decadence, but recognised by all as an icon of world tourism almost as famous as the Falls themselves, the Victoria Falls Hotel is the pride of Zimbabwe's tourist industry and steeped in a rich and interesting history. The Hotel owes its origins to the determined dream of one man, Cecil John Rhodes, and his ultimately unrealised vision for the development of a railway the length of the African continent, from Cape to Cairo. Rhodes developed his railway from the southern Cape northwards, reaching Bulawayo in 1897 and arriving at the banks of the Zambezi (alternatively spelt 'Zambesi' in many earlier references) in 1904.

Equipment and materials were quickly transported by train from Bulawayo for the construction of a simple hotel building, primarily to accommodate key railway personnel during the building of the Victoria Falls Bridge and continuation of the railway line north. Situated overlooking the Batoka Gorge below the Falls, the Hotel is positioned to face the grand view of the gorge, crossed by the Victoria Falls Bridge and with the rising spray of the Victoria Falls in the background. In those early days the gorges were romantically nicknamed the 'Corridors of Time,' after the discovery that they had been progressively eroded by the waters of the Zambezi over the millennia.

The original Victoria Falls Hotel boasted all the latest modern conveniences of the day, including electric lights, ceiling fans, hot and cold water and 'perfect sanitation.' Today the Hotel still offers all that one would expect from a first class five-star Hotel with a reputation for luxury and quality, supported by staff dedicated to the highest standards of service.

The Hotel's path through time to the present is the story of the development of modern travel and tourism, including the growth of two tourist towns, the birth of two independent countries and all influenced against a backdrop of global events, including one world-wide pandemic and two world wars.

Many who visit the Falls find themselves exploring the corridors of the Hotel, either intentionally or accidentally losing their way in the maze of interconnecting corridors whilst studying the archive photographs, posters and memorabilia from the early days of its history displayed along the walls. This book attempts to describe some of the events and bring to life the colourful characters involved in the story of this iconic Hotel, from humble beginnings through the corridors of time to the world-famous luxury Hotel we know today.

To the Victoria Falls

Known to the local inhabitants of the region for centuries, the majestic natural wonder of the Victoria Falls was first brought to the attention of the wider world by the famous Scottish missionary and explorer Dr David Livingstone (1813-1873).

In mid-1851 Livingstone and his travelling companion William Oswell were exploring north into the unmapped interior, eventually reaching a large river which the inhabitants living along its wide reaches called the *Liambai* and which Livingstone correctly identified as the Zambezi, previously known only to Europeans by its lower stretches and great delta on the east coast. Befriending the Makalolo chief Sebetwane, who held power in the region, they were told of a great waterfall some distance downstream, although they did not travel to visit them. Livingstone later recorded:

"Of these we had often heard since we came into the country; indeed, one of the questions asked by Sebituane was, 'Have you smoke that sounds in your country?' They [the Makalolo] *did not go near enough to examine them, but, viewing them with awe at a distance, said, in reference to the vapour and noise, 'Mosi oa Tunya' (smoke does sound there). It was previously called Shongwe, the meaning of which I could not ascertain."*

It was not until 1855, after first exploring upstream and a route across to the west coast, that Livingstone returned to the Zambezi with his Makalolo porters and finally journeyed downstream, escorted by Sebetwane's successor, Chief Sekeletu. Travelling by canoe and then walking along the north bank to avoid the Katambora Rapids, Sekeletu arranged a canoe and local boatman to take Livingstone the final distance downstream to the waterfall.

Dr David Livingstone (1813-1873)

On 16th November 1855 Livingstone was guided to a small island on the very lip of the Falls. Scrambling through vegetation to the sudden edge Livingstone struggled to understand the dramatic scene which unfolded before him:

"I did not comprehend it until, creeping with awe to the verge, I peered down into a large rent which had been made from bank to bank of the broad Zambesi, and saw that a stream of a thousand yards [915 m] broad leaped down a hundred feet [30.5 m]... the most wonderful sight I had witnessed in Africa."

Livingstone was perhaps deliberately cautious in his estimates, adding: *"Whoever may come after me will not, I trust, have reason to say I have indulged in exaggeration"* (Livingstone, 1857). He seriously underestimated the scale of the Falls, which span 1,708 metres (5,604 feet or 1,868 yards) and drop up to 108 metres (355 feet).

On his explorations Livingstone carefully recorded local names for geographic landmarks. Here, however, he also named them in English in honour of his monarch, the reigning British Queen Victoria.

"Being persuaded that Mr Oswell and myself were the very first Europeans who ever visited the Zambesi in the centre of the country, and that this is the connecting link between the known and unknown portions of that river, I decided to use the same liberty as the Makololo did, and gave the only English name I have affixed to any part of the country." (Livingstone, 1857)

Livingstone continued his epic journey following the Zambezi downstream to the east coast, again supported by his Makalolo porters, and completing a 3,000 mile (4,828 km) trek from the west to east coasts of the continent in the process. Returning to England Livingstone's accounts of his African travels caught the imagination of Victorian Britain. His first book, 'Missionary Travels and Researches in South Africa' was published in 1857 and became an instant best-seller. Livingstone envisioned the Zambezi River as the transport route by which the central regions of Africa would be opened up to Christian values and trade, describing the Zambezi as 'God's Highway.' But his dreams of 'Christianity, Commerce and Civilisation' - his personal motto - were dashed by the impassable gorges and rapids of the Middle Zambezi sections below the Victoria Falls.

Many followed in Livingstone's footsteps to the Falls. Yet few predicted that within fifty years of Livingstone first setting sight on the great waterfall that they would be connected to the Cape by rail and the gorges below traversed by the highest railway bridge in the world.

Rhodes and Rail

Cecil John Rhodes (1853-1902) arrived at the Cape Colony in September 1870 at the age of 17. After a short unsuccessful stint cotton farming, he followed his older brother Herbert to the newly discovered diamond fields in Kimberley, where he was to have slightly better luck. Rhodes made his fortune at Kimberley, founding the De Beers Consolidated Mining Company in 1888.

Rhodes was an ardent believer in British colonial imperialism, and as the vehicle for his ambitions he formed the British South Africa Company (B.S.A.C.), seeking British Royal approval for its activities in southern Africa. The Royal Charter, granted by Queen Victoria in 1889, gave the Company authority to administer an unspecified area of southern Africa on behalf of the British government.

The Charter bestowed wide-ranging powers to the Company, including:

"The right to make and maintain roads, railways, telegraphs, harbours; to carry on mining or other industries; to carry on lawful commerce; to settle territories and promote immigration; to establish or authorize banking companies; to develop, improve, clear, plant and irrigate land; to establish and maintain agencies in Our Colonies and Possessions, and elsewhere; to grant lands in terms of years or in perpetuity." (Strage, 1974)

These powers, however, were conditional on the agreement of appropriate, and

Railway construction

legitimate, treaties with local rulers - but merely a paperwork exercise for a man of Rhodes' means and methods. Rhodes became Prime Minister of the British Cape Colony in 1890 and championed the railway as the essential means by which to achieve his political and business ambitions. He is recorded as saying: *"Pure philanthropy is all very well in its way, but philanthropy plus five per cent is a good deal better"* (Hensman, 1901).

Rhodesia was officially named after him in May 1895, a reflection of his popularity as the territory had already become widely known as 'Zambesia.' The less appealing 'Charterland' had also been in widely used. The territory north of the Zambezi was originally divided into North-Western and North-Eastern Rhodesia, before being amalgamated to form Northern Rhodesia in 1911 (and known as Zambia since independence in 1964). The name of Southern Rhodesia (known as Zimbabwe since independence in 1980) was officially adopted in 1898 for the territory south of the Zambezi (Northern Rhodesia Journal, January 1956).

Cape to Cairo

After initial successes at Kimberley, Rhodes briefly returned to Oxford to complete his studies, becoming friends with Sir Charles Metcalfe (1853-1928). In 1878 Metcalfe joined the firm of Sir Douglas Fox and Partners and later travelled to South Africa as their consulting engineer for the developing Cape railway system, where he renewed his friendship with Rhodes. Sir Charles would spend three decades as the company's chief representative in southern Africa.

As early as 1888 Sir Charles had envisaged an 'African Trunk Line' - a rail and communications route traversing the length of the continent. The grand concept soon became popularly known as the 'Cape to Cairo' railway, the 'iron spine and ribs of Africa.' At the time several European powers were competing in their rush to claim African territories, and the Portuguese and German powers in particular looked towards the regions of the Upper Zambezi in order to connect territories on the east and west coasts. Sir Charles advised in an article he co-authored and published in London *"there is positively a race for the interior, and that nothing but a firm policy will maintain British interests and keep open the way for the development of British trade in Africa"* (Metcalfe and Richarde-Seaver, 1889).

Rhodes quickly became convinced of the importance of the railway in developing the 'British sphere of influence' in southern Africa. Although the Cape to Cairo scheme never materialised in its entirety, this period saw the rapid spread of a interconnected web of 'pioneer railways,' penetrating the subcontinent from the south and east coasts and opening up the interior to development.

The section of the railway line to Bulawayo was officially opened on 4th November 1897, to much ceremony and fanfare, with many dignitaries from all corners of the British Empire travelling by special train for the event. Cecil Rhodes, who did not attend the celebrations due to ill health, sent a telegram announcing;

"We are bound, and I have made up my mind, to go on to the Zambesi without delay. We have magnificent coalfields lying between here and there, which means a great deal to us engaged in the practical workings of railways. Let us see it on the Zambesi during our lifetime. It will be small consolation to me and to you to know it will be there when we are dead and gone." (White, 1973)

Rhodes became seduced by the romance of the railway crossing the river just below the natural wonder of the Victoria Falls, and he is quoted to have said *"Build the bridge across the Zambezi where the trains, as they pass, will catch the spray of the Falls,"* although no-one is quite sure when or to whom he gave this instruction.

Rhodes has always been a polarizing figure, dividing opinion in his day, and even more so when judged by modern standards and perspectives. The railway into the interior and the Bridge over the Zambezi are, however, his great legacy to the commercial, industrial and economic development of southern Africa. It would be four years, however, before the extension north was commissioned, in 1901, and another three before the railway reached the Zambezi, a year after Rhodes had himself passed away, having never visited the Falls.

The Old Drift

Prior to the building of the Victoria Falls Bridge, the Zambezi River was crossed above the Victoria Falls at several established ferry points. Travellers would head for the Big Tree, the huge baobab tree close to the river above the Falls (and still standing to this day), to make arrangements to cross the river. Many early explorers, hunters and missionaries travelled this route north into the territory known as Barotseland (part of modern-day Zambia).

The most important crossing was nine kilometres upstream of the Falls, where the river was at its narrowest, about a kilometre in width, and also at its deepest. Known as the Old Drift, a small European settlement of the same name slowly established itself on the north bank to await the arrival of the railway, which they confidently assumed would have to cross the river close by. Mr Frederick J 'Mopane' Clarke arrived at the banks of the Zambezi in late 1898, charged with operating the crossing and associated forwarding services on behalf of the

The Old Drift Mission Station (right) built by Coisson in 1900

Chartered Company. A skilled carpenter, 'Mopane' Clarke established what would become the core of the new settlement, a small 'hotel' built of wood and mud, and adjacent bar. Within a couple of years several trading stores and bars had sprung up, including a Mission Station founded by an Italian, Giovanni Daniele Augusto Coisson (under the auspices of the Paris Missionary Society) and associated school.

Clarke operated the crossing using an iron barge transported in sections to the Zambezi in mid-1898, and later also a steam launch. Passengers were taken in the barge, paddled by eight Barotse men, whilst wagons and goods were towed by the launch. The choice of site, however, was not ideal for a settlement - too close to the river, it became a flat marshy quagmire in the wet season and proved extremely unhealthy. By the end of 1901 the decision had been made to relocate the Company's administration offices, including the Post Office, to a healthier location away from the river and on the higher sand belt. Known as Constitution Hill the site would soon become the nucleus of the new pioneer town of Livingstone (Roberts, 2020a).

Mr Clark Stakes His Claim

In May 1903 Percy Missen Clark arrived at the Victoria Falls from Bulawayo with the intention of starting a photography business.

"I made my headquarters at the Old Drift for the time being, but my intention

was to settle at Victoria Falls as soon as the railway was completed, for I believed that there would be great opportunities for those who got in early at the railhead. At the end of the year I engaged a man to build a hut for me near the spot where the railway station would be pitched, and where the hotel would be built, but I had no mind to cross the river until the railway did come up.

Percy Clark outside his photography hut

"While I lived at the Old Drift I spent a lot of my time at the Victoria Falls taking photographs, and I got together quite a good collection. I would camp out for a couple of days at a time in the hut... When that was completed I lived in it, but for most of the time I was over on the other side at the Old Drift. I liked the older haunts, and the old crowd." (Clark, 1936)

Despite claiming to be the first resident of what would become Victoria Falls town, Clark kept one foot on the north bank and still thought of himself as 'an Old Drifter.' He lived in the Falls area until his death in 1937 - but is buried, however, in Livingstone Cemetery, together with his wife, Kate.

Clark's primary trade was photography, selling a variety of postcards and a popular portfolio of photographs of the Falls entitled a 'Souvenir of the Victoria Falls,' of which there were several variations. He also developed his own guidebook to the Falls, of which there are several editions, and traded in a variety of African curios and souvenirs.

Another individual with a foothold on the south bank was Albert Giese, who had established a series of trading stores between Wankie (now Hwange) and Victoria Falls, including one a short distance upstream of the Falls and close to the 'Big Tree.' Giese also operated a short-lived ferry service across the river to the northern bank, the nearest river crossing to the Falls.

The Railway Arrives

Construction of the final 68 mile (109.5 km) section of the railway line to Victoria Falls began on 21st September 1903, again financed by Railway Company, who were also responsible for the funding of the Bridge.

The first 47 miles (75.5 km) of line from Hwange was particularly challenging for the construction gangs, and included very heavy work through difficult country covered in dense bush and supporting a full complement of Africa's 'Big Five.' Percy Clark had travelled to the Falls whilst the railway was still under construction, recording that the workmen slept in the trees for fear of attack from lion and other dangerous wild animals.

Despite these difficulties, the line to the Victoria Falls was completed on 24th April 1904. As the last rails were laid the supporting construction train slowly rolled to a stop within sight of the rising spray of the Victoria Falls. Celebrations were held including a sports-day and feast for all the construction workers. In his autobiography Percy Clark proudly tells of his success in selling photographs of the arrival of the first train to all the engineers, contractors and railway staff, recording that he *"did a roaring trade in prints at five shillings a time"* (Clark, 1936).

A temporary station building was quickly improvised, with the Construction Company operating two trains a week between Hwange and Victoria Falls from

The first construction train to reach the Falls

10th May 1904, before the line was handed over to the Railway Company for official opening on 20th June 1904 (a permanent station building was erected in the first half of 1905 with Mr John Fairlamb as Station Master).

The distance from Cape Town was 1,641 miles (2,641 kilometres). Only twenty years before it took over six months of trekking with oxen to get to the Falls - now the journey was measured in days. The trains took 22 hours on the Bulawayo to Victoria Falls journey and 24 hours on the return. In advertisements it was stressed that passengers needed to provide their own blankets and food for their journey as there were no dining carriages and no intermediate stations where refreshments could be obtained. Mr Pierre Gavuzzi, Manager of the Bulawayo Grand Hotel, provided hampers for the adventurous train travellers. A rail dining service was eventually introduced in October 1905.

The Grand Hotel, opened in 1899, was managed by the business partnership of Mr G Estran and Mr W Scott-Rodger. Fellow Italians, Estran and Gavuzzi met whilst working under César Ritz and Auguste Escoffier at the acclaimed Savoy and Carlton Hotels in London during the 1890s. Both men trained in France, during which time Gavuzzi appears to have adopted the name Pierre, being born Pietro Carlo Gavuzzi in Monticello, Italy, in 1870 (Stewart, 2010). Gavuzzi was a popular character and famed locally for his fine strawberries (grown on a plot of land which would later become the Prince's Theatre), encouraging his patrons to dine to live music and introducing table-tennis, in the form of 'ping-pong,' to Rhodesia - presumably much-needed entertainment for his guests.

> *"He soon had Bulawayo talking about the excellence of his cuisine and before long it not only became fashionable to attend banquets at the Grand, but the 'Bulawayo Chronicle' would also publish the menu in full the following day."*
> (Rhodesia Railways Magazine, December 1954)

In late May 1904 Mr Gavuzzi would have been arranging his own hamper for the journey north, travelling by train with a large party of workmen and materials destined for the construction of a hotel overlooking the rising spray of the Falls.

The Zambezi Express

The Victoria Falls Hotel

With the line to the Falls complete the Railway Company arranged in early May 1904 for the transportation of materials for the construction of a 'temporary' hotel at the Falls.

"The material for the temporary building to be erected at Victoria Falls Station for the accommodation of travellers has been despatched." (Bulawayo Chronicle, May 1904)

It has previously been recorded that the Victoria Falls Hotel opened on 8th June 1904 (Creewel, 2004), and this may well have been the original planned opening date. A notice in the Bulawayo Chronicle of 4th June, however, appears to indicate that construction of the Hotel was still ongoing, with a party of workmen departing for the Falls on Monday, 30th May.

"A large party of workmen left by last Monday's train to the north to complete the erection of the Victoria Falls Hotel. It has been rumoured that only a temporary structure is being put up, and by this description of the hotel many people fancy it will provide but poor accommodation..."

A notice from the Railway Company appeared in the same issue indicating a three week delay in construction:

"A telegram has been received from Mr S F Townsend, of the Rhodesia Railways, notifying that visitors would do well to defer their trips for about three weeks in consequence of delay in the hotel construction." (Bulawayo Chronicle, June 1904)

The Hotel was described as a temporary structure, to house the chief railway contractors, consultants and other eminent visitors involved with the development of the Bridge and railway. As such, many assumed it was to be dismantled and removed from the site once the concentration of railway construction moved north. Temporary, from the Railway Company's perspective however, appears to have meant until grander, more permanent facilities could be erected.

A simple wood and iron structure, construction of the Hotel was speedily effected once construction materials and men arrived at the Falls. The main building consisted of a cast-iron frame, wooden panels and corrugated iron roof, all raised above the ground and fronted with a wide open veranda overlooking the Batoka Gorge, the view extending down to the Bridge site and rising spray of the Falls.

The first Victoria Falls Hotel

The Hotel was initially capable of hosting 20 guests at a time, with twelve single and four double rooms, together with a dining room, bar and offices, and was equipped with modern luxuries such as electric lights and fans and running hot and cold water. One of the specialist engineers sent out by the Bridge Company, Howard Longbottom, assisted with the installation of the electrical fittings.

The Railway Company leased the operation and management of the Hotel to the partnership of Mr G Estran and Mr W Scott-Rodger, who transferred Mr Pierre Gavuzzi from Bulawayo to oversee the establishment and operation of the new Hotel.

The early Hotel staff were cosmopolitan in origins - Mr Gavuzzi was Italian, the chef French, and the barman from Chicago, with service supported by Indian waiters. The young chef, Mr Marcel Mitton, known as 'the Frenchman who became a Rhodesian,' would become a famous figure in early Rhodesian history, trying his hand as a hunter and miner as well as a chef.

"The management will be under the direct supervision of M Pierre Gavuzzi, of the Grand Hotel, Bulawayo, and he will have a staff of competent assistants, trained under him. A first-class French chef, a Chicago barman, Arab waiters and white attendants will be found at this hotel. The cuisine will be as fine as experience can make it... Electric light is being installed throughout. Each of the tables in the dining room will be lighted by separate standards, so as to lend a softness to the illumination of the room. Refrigerators, cold chambers and ice will certainly be appreciated in the climate of the Victoria Falls, and will allow of the finest meat and vegetables being kept for the table. Bathrooms with beautiful fixed baths, with hot and cold water, will also be found in this

latest example of Rhodesian enterprise and to counteract any great heat in the summer, electric fans will be running to cool the atmosphere. M Gavuzzi has gone to the Falls, but he is not leaving us for good. He will still retain the management of the Grand Hotel, Bulawayo." (Bulawayo Chronicle, June 1904)

After the delays in construction there appears have been no grand opening celebration, although the Hotel appears to have been opened at the same time as the official opening of the railway line to the Falls on 20th June. An advert from early July indicates the Hotel was already proving popular.

"In consequence of the great demand for rooms at the Victoria Falls Hotel, P Gavuzzi notifies intending visitors that they should advise him of the date of their arrival in order to ensure accommodation and to avoid disappointment. Travellers should be well prepared with blankets for the train journey." (Bulawayo Chronicle, July 1904)

The lowest all-inclusive tariff was twelve shillings six pence per day. Many of the Hotel's early guests would have been linked to the Railway Company preparing for the continuing construction of the railway line and completion of the Bridge, no doubt including Sir Charles Metcalfe, as well as the occasional adventurous traveller. The earliest known guest recorded as staying at the Hotel, Dr Arthur E Healy, a travelling dentist from Rockland, Maine, arrived on the first through train to the Falls on the 28th June.

"Dr. Healy was the only American on the first through train to Victoria Falls, and was the first American to register at the Victoria Falls Hotel on its opening in 1904." (American Dental Journal, 1906)

The first Victoria Falls Hotel, with railway line in left foreground

It is also recorded that one of the early visitors to stay at the Hotel, appropriately, was Mrs Agnes Bruce, David Livingstone's daughter, fifty years after her famous father first set sight on the Falls. Percy Clark claimed to have had the first meal served at the Hotel:

"I had the first meal that was served to a customer at the Victoria Falls Hotel. I ate it, I remember, in an annexe to the coal-hole near the kitchen. It was lunch... and I paid about four shillings for it." (Clark, 1936)

The rising numbers of visitors to the Falls did not go unnoticed by the Railway Company, Sir Charles Metcalfe and others soon referring to the Hotel in terms of accommodating recreational visitors rather than railway engineers.

"The line has been open right up to the Victoria Falls since June 20th, and the Hotel we have built there for the accommodation of visitors is a very comfortable one. It possesses every modern convenience, and from it there is obtained a beautiful view of the Zambezi Gorge." (Metcalfe, 1904)

Guest lists from late 1904 show people arriving from England, the United States and the Cape Colony. It soon became clear that the Hotel needed increased capacity to accommodate the growing number of guests, with visitors often having to use train carriages as extra accommodation at busy periods. In September 1904 two old railway sheds were relocated to the site, with one - previously used as an engine shed at Mandegos (later renamed Vila Pery, and now called Chimoio) on the narrow gauge line from Beira on the east coast - converted into a large dining room, and the other into bedrooms. Soon after further railway buildings were added, re-purposed into accommodation with en suite bathrooms and becoming known as the Annex or Honeymoon Suites.

The Hotel and Annex buildings

"The Hotel, at the beginning, was simply a long structure of wood and iron containing a dining room and bar, bedrooms and offices. Later on it was enlarged by the addition of two large engine sheds removed from railway headquarters. One of these was converted into a dining room and the other into bedrooms. Later still two annexes of wood and iron were put up, complete with bathrooms. In the hot weather the rooms were ovens, and in the cold, refrigerators - but nobody grumbled much. After all, what could one expect in the heart of Africa?" (Clark, 1936)

The Hotel's first logo included the African lion and Egyptian sphinx, symbolising Rhodes' dream of a railway connecting Africa from the Cape to Cairo, and fittingly readopted by the Hotel since 1996.

First Train Tourists

The first group of railway tourists known to travel to the Victoria Falls from Cape Town arrived on a specially booked private train in late June 1904, the first through train to the Zambezi. The trip was organised by a Mr Arderne, a businessman based in the Cape, who hired the Cape Railway's Train de Luxe, complete with refrigerator truck and dining car.

The party arrived at the Falls on 28th June 1904 after a journey of six days. They stayed six nights, and such was the luxury of the train that they ate and slept aboard, despite the Victoria Falls Hotel being open for business (although unable to accommodate the whole group of over 30 visitors). After a quick initial visit to the Falls the members of the party returned to the luxury of their train, which they had grandly nicknamed the 'Victoria Falls Railway Carriage Hotel.'

"Then there was a busy hour, many of us writing letters, sending telegrams announcing our arrival, and postcards to friends, which had been specially brought to be posted here, that they might bear the stamp of the Victoria Falls post office. One young lady was so anxious to have such a card that she addressed one to herself to her Cape Town home."

Reference was made by one visitor of plans for a grander five-storey building to be built the following year.

"A hundred yards away from our halting place today, is the site of the Victoria Falls Hotel which may be built next year, and according to the published plan is to be a delightful five-story building with ample verandas from which grand views of the Falls can be obtained." (Lyon, 1904)

The Arderne party gather for Sunday morning service

Quinine was served daily at breakfast and the chef devised a special customised menu with themed names, including a Victoria Falls pudding with 'spray effect.' The women in the group were carried through the Rainforest in suspended hammocks and explored the islands on the river above the Falls by canoe and launch. On the train was a piano - the first one ever to be heard at the Falls (Green, 1968).

After several days fully exploring the north and south banks of the Falls and river upstream, their last full day at the Falls saw the party gathering at the temporary railway station for a Sunday morning service.

"With no church bells but the distant booming of the Falls to call us to prayers, we assembled at eleven o'clock on the stoep of the Station to worship God. Our service was a bright and impressive one, the address earnest, thoughtful and poetical, leaving in each heart a longing for higher and better things. Service ended, many of the party strolled on to the stoep of the newly-erected hotel to admire from this vantage ground the beautiful view of the Zambesi river, winding its tortuous way through its narrow channel, walled in on both sides by grand rugged, rocky cliffs. The situation of this hotel for scenic effect is perfect, and many a traveller, I feel sure, will leave with innumerable regrets a spot so fitted to satisfy his love of the beautiful." (Lyon, 1904)

The party departed for Bulawayo by train the following morning, 4th July, beginning their long journey south to the Cape. A descriptive account of this inaugural tour, written by various of the participants and illustrated with many photographs, was published privately in Cape Town as a souvenir (Lyon, 1904).

Hotel Farm Gardens

An area of the land beyond the Railway Station was developed into the Hotel's farm gardens, managed by Mr Gavuzzi with the aim of supplying fresh produce for the kitchens, and again growing his prized strawberries.

"In the gardens are melons, pines [pineapples], tomatoes, tobacco, asparagus, beans, peas, potatoes, cucumbers, celery, lettuce, weighing 6½ lbs. (salade romaine), radishes, and strawberries, while there are 4,000 cabbages, some weighing 18 lbs. [over 8 kg]... Mr Pierre Gavuzzi was never at rest, and was a tireless worker for the comfort of his guests." (South Africa Handbook, 1905)

Day trippers could order lunch hampers from the Hotel to be delivered to pre-arranged picnic spots around the Falls.

Mysterious Disappearance

Soon after opening a strange incident occurred at the Hotel, recounted by Gavuzzi:

"Eight or nine months ago a man, aged about 45, came to the Hotel, saying he was from Kimberley. He was a silent, lonely, but not gloomy man. During the six days he was at the Hotel he always repelled offers to be shown round. He said he did not want to hear anybody speaking when he was looking at the Falls, but just to go and see the effect they had on him alone...

"On the seventh day he went out as usual, and he never returned. No trace of him has ever been discovered. His luggage is still at the Hotel along with a riding whip, but it has not led to any identification of the man who shortly after leaving the Hotel apparently quitted the world." (South Africa Handbook No.34, 1905)

Royal Visitors

Her Royal Highness Princess Helena, daughter of Queen Victoria and also known by her married title of Princess Christian of Schleswig-Holstein, and her elder daughter Princess Victoria, known as Princess Helena Victoria, were the first members of the British Royal Family to visit the Victoria Falls on 16th September 1904. Lord and Lady Roberts also visited the Falls at the same time. Rickshaws were sent up from Bulawayo to convey the Royal guests to and from the Falls.

Percy Clark recalled the visit:

"The first great lady of the many I have met at the Falls was Princess Christian. She came by special train in 1904, and I was commanded to bring post cards and photographs to the royal train for her inspection. In those rough-and-ready days few of us had complete suits to our names, and I was in like case with the majority. I was in a quandary. I couldn't very well appear before her Royal Highness in khaki slacks and a shirt, so I hunted round the camp to collect what decent togs I could borrow or steal... until at last I had the complete outfit in which to present myself to Royalty... but when I told the aide-de-camp afterwards about my search for a rig-out he roared with laughter. He told the Princess the story subsequently, and I heard that it amused her hugely." (Clark, 1936)

Princess Christian recorded that she was *"deeply impressed with the Victoria Falls, and that no one coming to South Africa should miss seeing them"* (British South Africa Company, 1907).

Princess Christian's younger daughter, Princess Marie-Louise, visited the Falls in the mid-1920s. In her autobiography, the Princess simply recorded: *"We stayed at the Victoria Falls for a few days in a very comfortable hotel"* (Creewel, 2004).

Visit of Lord and Lady Roberts

Lord and Lady Roberts, together with their two daughters, the Ladies Aileen and Edwina Roberts, visited the Falls almost immediately after the Royal Princesses. Field Marshal Lord Frederick Sleigh Roberts, Earl of Kandahar, was at the time one of the most distinguished and celebrated commanders in the British Army, having served in India, Abyssinia (Ethiopia) and Afghanistan (most notably the Battle of Kandahar in September 1880) before leading British Forces in the latter half of the Second Anglo-Boer War.

"In September 1904, the whole family, accompanied by Major Furse as A.D.C. [aide-de-camp], went on three month's tour of South Africa. They landed at Cape Town and went straight up country to see the Victoria Falls. Here they had the incomparable thrill of crossing directly over the gorge in a cage on a wire span. Roberts himself was lost for words of description, as are most who see that fabulous sight. Not so, though, Lady Roberts' old maid, who described them as 'sweetly pretty.'" (James, 1954)

Lord and Lady Roberts said they were *"astonished at the grandeur of the Falls, which surpass in natural majesty anything else they have ever seen"* (British South Africa Company, 1907).

Lord Roberts and party at the Victoria Falls Hotel

The British South Africa Company's Directors report dated 6th November 1905 recorded:

"In commemoration of the visit of Her Royal Highness Princess Christian and Princes Victoria of Schlewig Holstein and Lord and Lady Roberts, three of the largest islands just above the Falls have been named 'Princess Christian,' 'Princess Victoria' and 'Kandahar.'" (Northern Rhodesia Journal, July 1953)

A Visit to the Falls

An early account of visit to the Hotel appeared in the Bulawayo Chronicle in October 1904. The author names a Mr Pregno, who appears to have been responsible for guest services at the Hotel.

"No visitor to the Victoria Falls, not even the most unimaginative, can help being struck with the changes which have taken place there recently. To the average traveller of a year ago, the Falls were somewhere in regions accessible only after a long journey involving much discomfort and many hardships, and a visit was a event hardly to be dreamed of. To-day the resident in Bulawayo arranges to spend a week-end in the journey to and from the Falls and only leaves his business for a matter of four or five days to do the round trip. He enters a comfortable railway carriage here, and within twenty-four hours he can step out of the train, and five minute's walk will being him to the edge of the Zambesi and - the Falls.

"There is a modern and up-to-date hotel where the traveller can make as pleasant a stay as if he were in any first-class English residence. Last week I had the pleasure of spending some six days at the Victoria Falls Hotel, and to the unfailing courtesy and attention of Mr Pregno, I attribute a most pleasant and enjoyable time.

Early Hotel luggage label

"The Hotel is situated about 50 yards [45.7m] from the railway station. Its position was selected, I believe, with the double object of being close to the railway stations, besides commanding an excellent view of the Falls. The building is raised several feet from the ground and contains over forty rooms, half of which are on the Hotel frontage and are separated from the remaining twenty by a long and roomy passage. A broad verandah of about 100 feet [30.5m] in length contributes greatly towards the general comfort and is most suitable for an evening stroll and chat just before turning in for the night. One would not expect that the whole hotel would be fitted up with electric light or that ice would be manufactured there, but, notwithstanding the very heavy cost to the management, it possesses both these conveniences. An excellent billiard table is provided for those who wield the cue and even at the Victoria Falls Hotel I have found those who rank as first-class players in the London clubs...

"We made up a nice little family party that night at the Hotel and recounted our various experiences and adventures of the day. After that, the musical members entertained us and probably the lazy crocs and hippos on the river were somewhat astonished at the sound of distant laughter and merriment. The Misses Keen presided jointly at the piano. Miss D Keen delighted the hearts of everyone with a charming rendition of that old favourite 'Rhodesia is all the rage just now.' Mr Frank Trythall, too, kept us in roars of laughter, especially with his song, 'The Great Big Wheel.' Colonel Wyndham and Major McEwen of the 16th Lancers were also there, but they preferred to sit still and enjoy the fun. Our holiday came to an end far too soon for our liking. Fortunately, we had no accidents. I cannot permit myself to say anything of the beauty and grandeur of the Falls. It needs a cleverer man than myself to do that. I can only say, 'Go and see them.'" (Bulawayo Chronicle, October 1904)

The Victoria Falls Bridge

With the arrival of the railway heavy materials for the construction of the Victoria Falls Bridge could at last be transported to the site. The Bridge was designed by Mr George Andrew Hobson of London based consultants Sir Douglas Fox and Partners, and the steelwork manufactured by Cleveland Bridge & Engineering Company in Darlington, England, before being shipped to Beira and transported on the railway to Bulawayo and then on to the Victoria Falls.

The Cleveland Bridge Company appointed Georges C Imbault, a gifted young Frenchman, as their Chief Construction Engineer. Imbault established his camp on the north bank of the river a short distance above the Falls and in April 1904 he was joined by a small team of about 30 skilled construction engineers sent from England by the Cleveland Bridge Company for the construction work.

The Bridge is of a trussed arch design, the main arch a graceful parabolic curve with a rise of 90 feet (27.4 m) and span of 500 feet (152.4 m), with two short connecting side spans giving a total width of 650 feet (198.1 m). Erection of the side spans proved to be one of the biggest challenges in the construction.

Bridge engineers at work

Once complete (towards the end of 1904), construction of the main arch progressed rapidly, reaching outwards from each side of the gorge. The separate sides of the arch were supported as cantilevers by steel wire cables cut into the rock on either bank, and as the work proceeded daily observations were taken to see that the centre axis of the structure was maintained.

On the 31st March 1905 the main arches were ready to be joined, when it was found that the final sections overlapped by several centimetres. However, the chief construction engineer, Imbault, remained confident and the following morning, after the steelwork had cooled and contracted during the night, the final sections fitted perfectly.

The engineering company, Sir Douglas Fox and Partners, announced to the world that the arch of the great Zambezi Bridge was linked up at 6 o'clock on Saturday 1st April 1905. An engineering report details that there were anxious minutes as the sun rose and everyone watched to see if the effects of the heat on the steel, and tension of the whole structure, had been accurately calculated. By July construction of the steelwork arch was complete, with a temporary upper deck completed the following month, allowing the transportation of railway materials for the continuation of the railway line northwards (Roberts, 2020b).

Not everyone was in favour of the Bridge being constructed within view of the Falls, including Cecil Rhodes' brother, Frank. Mr Hobson, the designer of the Bridge, recalled:

The arches connected

"When at Victoria Falls [Hotel] last July (1905), I had many talks with one of the chief malcontents, the late Colonel Frank Rhodes... Looking at the bridge from our breakfast table, in his cheery way he said: 'Well, I have done all I could to prevent the bridge being built there; but there it is, and nothing is now left for me to do but pray daily for an earthquake.' But he confessed that he liked the thing itself very well." (Hobson, 1923)

The Iron and Timber

During the constructionn of the Victoria Falls Bridge an outside bar, known to the railway workers and bridge engineers as the 'Iron and Timber,' was provided at the Hotel, and soon became the social hub of the transitional community, with many an evening was described as 'lively.' Percy Clark expands in his autobiography:

"While the Bridge was still in course of construction an outside bar was put up for the workmen. They were a rough lot, even for the wilds, and they made the Hotel very uncomfortable for sedater guests in the main building, especially just after they got their monthly pay. At this time the Hotel was run by private management. The lessee was an Italian, and the antics of his customers, both heads and hands, kept him scared almost out of his wits... Whenever he came in sight of the workmen using the outside bar he was at once chased round the premises. If caught he was hauled into the bar and made to stand drinks all round. He did not relish this rough handling and had not the knack of taking it easily. He therefore gave the outside bar a wide berth, though he must have made a pile from it. For two or three days after the men received their pay the bar would be packed. Drinking and gambling went on continuously, with free entertainment day and night for anyone who cared for that sort of thing. There was always a fight going on outside the bar - and the workmen certainly could scrap. Fortunately for the management it had secured the services of an ex-prize fighter as barman. He was not a very big chap, but he stood no nonsense from the crowd." (Clark, 1936)

Mr Gavuzzi appears to have fancied himself as a singer, it being recorded that for the opening of the Bridge *"Gavuzzi added to the gaiety by singing Italian arias"* (Green, 1968). This may account for his 'popularity' among the engineers.

"On one occasion when the whole gang was having a vary hilarious night of it in the Hotel bar Gavuzzi, who was small in stature, was hoisted up on the mantelpiece and obliged to sing a song." (Croxton, 1982)

After the main arch of the Bridge had been connected, work focussed on the fixed riveting of the structure, which had been temporarily pinned during the construction. The electric powered riveting machines regularly fused the local power system, which also served the Hotel. It was even recorded that the workers would purposely fuse the power each evening, much to the Manager's frustration! This also caused problems for the Hotel's chef, Marcel Mitton, melting the ice blocks and putting his cold room out of action:

"When he was ready to cater for 50 V.I.P. guests of the British Association, 35 cattle carcases went off in the not-so-cold room... Said Marcel at the time: 'I only hope the vast quantities of liquor consumed glossed over the deficiencies in solid refreshment.'" (Black, 1976)

Mr Mitton added that in those early days there *"was a veritable mountain of empty bottles surrounding the back of the Victoria Falls Hotel."*

A Valuable Property

The value of the Victoria Falls as a potential tourism destination was soon recognised by the Chartered Company.

"In the Victoria Falls we possess a very valuable property, which is likely to promote materially the prosperity of the country. During the short period in which the railway to the Falls has been open, a large number of visitors has been attracted to them, and the tourist traffic which may be legitimately expected in the immediate future is likely to increase." (British South Africa Company, 1905)

At the Ordinary General Meeting of the Railway Company shareholders, held in London in 1905, a report was presented recording that:

"Lord Grey has told you that we have reached the Victoria Falls. We took over that line on June 20th [1904]... We have also, since then, effected what we call a temporary hotel which, however, is a very comfortable one. It has every modern convenience and accommodation for about forty people. It has most magnificent views of the bluff gorge. It has the electric light, cold storage, hot and cold water baths, and every modern luxury. It is run by a manager who was formerly at the Savoy and the Carlton hotels, and I am glad to say that everyone appreciates his efforts and that he has been well patronised since the Hotel opened." (Rhodesia Railways, 1905)

The immediate area around the Falls on the south bank, known as the Victoria

The Victoria Falls Railway Station

Falls Reserve, was fenced as part of a conservation plan in 1904. The area included the Falls Rainforest and extended upstream to the Big Tree, Palm Tree Ferry and inland to the track leading to the Old Drift crossing.

The Falls Hotel was built on land within the designated Railway Reserve, together with the Railway Station, Post Office (with a telegraph line connecting to Livingstone) and Percy Clark's house and trading huts. All were supplied with water from a small pumping station above the Devil's Cataract.

News reports in 1905 still referred to the Company's desire for a much grander Hotel at the Falls, referring to plans for the construction of a 'mammoth hotel' (The World's Work, February 1905). The plans were still being actively promoted in mid-1905, by which time the Hotel's capacity had been expanded to 80 guests.

"At the Falls themselves there is a Hotel where accommodation is provided for eighty guests. True, it is only a temporary building, but it will shortly be replaced by a permanent one." (Scientific American Magazine, June 1905)

Within Reach of the World

By 1905 the Falls were being promoted as a global tourism attraction, one South African travel brochure boldly declaring:

"The average man in the street has hardly yet realised that the Victoria Falls are within reach of anybody having a couple of months to spare. It is as easy too get from London to Bulawayo to-day as it is to get from London to New York, and the passenger with find himself quite as luxuriously accommodated as upon the trip across the herring pond." (South Africa Handbook No.32, 1905)

The Union Castle Mail Steamship Company, official mail carrier from the United Kingdom to the Cape Colony in South Africa, was intrinsically linked with the early development of the Rhodesias. The Company sailed from Southampton every Saturday, taking 17 days to reach the Cape. From there it took three days by train to Bulawayo and a further 22 hours to reach the Falls. It was not uncommon for passengers to travel this great distance only to stay a few nights at the Falls Hotel and then start their return journey. A 1905 promotional booklet produced by Union Castle Line encouraged travel to the Zambezi, 'the World's Riviera.'

Travel companies such as Thomas Cook and Pickfords promoted combined rail and liner travel deals to visit *"nature's greatest spectacle"* where the traveller could *"enjoy European luxury even here in the heart of Africa"* (McGregor, 2009).

The Zambezi Regatta

The first Zambezi Regatta was held on 12th June 1905 to celebrate the fiftieth anniversary year of Livingstone's first arrival at the Falls and the construction of the Bridge. The regatta was the highlight to three days of sporting events and celebrations aimed at promoting the accessibility of the Falls to the wider world. The regatta was held on a mile and a half (2.4 km) straight reach of water between Luanda Island (now known as Long Island) and the north bank, and the one-day event was attended by close to a thousand visitors, flooding the Falls, and the Hotel, with an unprecedented number of visitors.

A camp site and grandstand were set up at the finish line and the big race was the Zambezi Four-Oared Championship. Crews from Cape Town, Port Elizabeth, and East London competed, and after a fine race East London came in winners with Cape Town second and Port Elizabeth third.

In the other races the crews of six were mostly made up of European settlers - one was comprised of Company employees and another with settlers from the Drift. The event was also notable for several 'native races' in traditional dugout canoes. It was said that the Paramount Chief, Lewanika, told his crew that if they did not win, he would leave them on an island in the Zambezi for the benefit of the crocodiles!

Percy Clark was less than impressed with the rush on local supplies:

"By the second day the Hotel was cleared of beer and whisky, and food had almost run out. I was invited by a friend to dine there. The feast was worthy of the rude fellow's grace: 'Gawd! What a meal!' I wished I had invited my friend to my own place. The service was terrible, with a wait of twenty minutes between each of the courses. These were: soup - with the taste and appearance of weak Bovril; one bony cutlet and half a potato; biscuits and cheese with no

Regatta grandstand

butter. There wasn't a scrap of butter in the Hotel, no joints, no poultry. For this magnificent (!) spread we were charged seven-and-six apiece. I'd sooner have bought a marriage licence. Along the regatta course were the usual 'joints' - poker tables, 'Under and Over, 'Crown and Anchor,' canteens, and the side-shows. The concessionaires, so to call them, must have raked in pots of money." (Clark, 1936)

There were apparently ugly scenes at the 'outside bar' of the Hotel when supplies of beer and whisky ran out and the last bottles were emptied. Green recalls interviewing Jack, later Colonel, Rose, one of the Cape rowers.

"It was a wild and exciting place in those days... Fever was a constant menace and there were few amenities but we enjoyed ourselves. There was lots to talk about - a bull hippo entered the marquee near the river where the boating club dinner was being held. We all cleared out pretty quick." (Green, 1968)

Green also records that it was during the regatta that a crocodile tried to enter one of the rooms of the Hotel, presumably disturbed by all the activity along the river. Hippopotamus have always been a hazard on the river, easily capable of capsizing a canoe and to be treated with utmost respect and caution.

"Several bad accidents have taken place already through these ugly denizens of the river charging boats. Two or three days before I arrived, while Mr Gavuzzi and a crew were rowing about a hippo tore a hole in the bottom of the boat, which immediately began to sink. The occupants had all to swim for it, but the distance to shore being only about 20 yards [18m]*, they got off with nothing worse than a ducking."* (South Africa Handbook No.34, 1905)

Incidents such as this resulted in a 'thinning' of the hippopotamus population prior to the Regatta.

The East London crew, regatta winners

South Bank Services

A new business partnership, Mr E Goodwin and Mr G Walker, were successful in securing a licence to operate boating services from the southern bank, servicing Hotel guests and other travellers. In August 1905 they announced the arrival of a new motor-launch on the river.

"Messrs Goodwin and Walker, the boat and coach proprietors on the South Bank, have this week added to the craft of the Upper Zambesi a smart and comfortable motor launch, which is named the 'Hinemoa,' after a famous Maori princess. The firm are to be congratulated on their enterprising venture, which will no doubt prove a sound investment; and whilst contributing in no small degree to the enjoyment of visitors will lend an additional feature of interest to life on the river.

"The new craft will seat about a dozen people and has a speed of about seven knots an hour [13 km/h]. In this connection I understand it is the intention of the Government to blast a channel through the shoals above the Falls, for the facilitating of the river traffic, and so lessen the risks of damage to boats on this delectable stretch of the Zambesi." (Bulawayo Chronicle, August 1905a)

In the first 'official' guide to the Falls, written by Mr Francis (Frank) William Sykes, Conservator and District Commissioner for the Falls on the north bank, the 'Victoria Falls Coach and Boating Company,' advertised their business as 'Motor Launch, Boat and Cart Proprietors.'

"Visitors conveyed to the many points of interest, including Cataract and Livingstone Islands. Picnic, fishing and shooting parties provided for. Visitors can arrange for the above with us at the Victoria Falls Hotel." (Sykes, 1905)

A Return to the Falls

Mr (later Sir) Ralph Williams, Resident Commissioner in Bechuanaland (1901-6), visited the Falls with his wife in August 1905, travelling by train and staying at the Falls Hotel. It was exactly twenty-three years after his first visit in 1883, with his wife and four year old son, in a journey by ox-wagon which had taken six months.

"I made many train journeys, the most interesting being my return in 1905 to the Victoria Falls. On the 14th of August 1883 I first visited the Falls, as I have already told. On the 14th of August 1905 I revisited them, to find there (for crowds now travelled thither) all the conveniences of civilisation. The great

Bridge was nearly finished, though part of it was still unplanked, the rails being laid over a yawning gulf of six hundred feet [182.8 m]. My wife and I crossed this on a trolley, and I confess that I was never more frightened in my life as the shaky and insecure little rattle-trap... threatened every moment to capsize. The engineers and all concerned crossed it in a dozen different ways all day long, and wandered through its mazes above and below as though strolling in Piccadilly, but to the uninitiated it was a fearsome task, and we were glad when we got safely back.

"It was very sad going over the old ground, for although the Chartered Company had done all that was possible to conserve the natural beauties, the mark of the beast was everywhere, the beast being the ubiquitous tourist. Even on Livingstone Island, on the very verge of the famous gorge, the ground was littered with the papers of a previous picnic party, and it seemed as though visitors positively tried to ruin the place." (Williams, 1913)

Official Opening of the Bridge

The official opening ceremony for the Victoria Falls Bridge took place on 12th September 1905. One of the newest 7th Class engines in the country at the time, decorated with two flags (that of the Chartered Company and the British Union Flag), palm leaves and floral dressings, pulled the six coaches which then halted on the Bridge for the passengers to alight. Mr Allan Bowes is recorded as the driver. The party was met by Sir Charles Metcalfe and Major (later Sir) Robert Coryndon, the first Administrator of North-Western Rhodesia (from 1900-07).

Sir Charles made the welcoming speech and invited Professor (later Sir) George H Darwin, son of Charles Darwin and President of the British Association for the Advancement of Science (now the British Science Association), to declare the Victoria Falls Bridge officially open. The Association had been invited to visit the Falls and open the Bridge as an extension to their tour of South Africa, with Professor Darwin describing the honour of opening the Bridge as the *"crowning glory of the tour."*

With the opening ceremony complete the train slowly drew forward amid cheers. The main group of guests alighted on the northern bank where they could explore the Palm Grove or visit Livingstone Island. The remainder of the guests visited the Rain Forest, under the guidance of Mr Allen, and then back to the Hotel for lunch, by which time the train returned with the first group and collected the second group for the trip to the north bank.

Opening of the Victoria Falls Bridge

Guests were given voucher tickets for the train, tours and meals, issued together with a special commemorative programme. In the evening the Hotel served dinner for a several hundred guests, after which trips to see the Falls by moonlight were offered. Among the distinguished guests was Mrs Agnes Livingstone Bruce, wife of Colonel Alexander Low Bruce and the eldest daughter of Dr David Livingstone.

Professor Darwin noted in an album of comments collected by Mr Gavuzzi

"I think the Victoria Falls the most beautiful and interesting sight I have ever seen. My only regret is that I have had so short a time available for seeing the place. The hospitality which we have received has exceeded anything I could have believed possible and it is rendered the more memorable to me from my having had the honour of formally opening the great Bridge."

Another visitor, identified only as 'R S B' wrote: *"To stand on the Hotel stoep and view Nature's magnificent spectacle and man's marvel of ingenuity in the great Bridge is an advantage possessed by no other Hotel in the world, and appreciated correspondingly by members of the British Association."*

Admiral Sir William James Lloyd Wharton, who died of typhoid in Cape Town on the return journey, commented:

"I have been full of admiration for everything I have seen here. Nature is at her best, while man has in this short time done marvels for the convenience of visitors. The comforts of this Hotel are complete and unexpected." (South Africa Handbook No.34, 1905)

Only Professor Darwin and the most distinguished guests had rooms at the Hotel, with many guests being accommodated on the train carriages. The British archaeologist and anthropologist Henry Balfour made the first of his four visits to the Victoria Falls for the opening ceremony, staying on one of the supporting trains.

> *"Had to dine late owing to the fearful crush. Food vile, so dined on bread and marmalade."* (Balfour, 1905)

After the crowds had left by special train the following day Balfour was upgraded to a room *"in the long building"* of the Hotel.

End of the Drift

It soon became apparent that the location of the Bridge and route of the railway would make the Old Drift crossing, and settlement, redundant - irrelevant of the health concerns over the site. After much consideration, including exploring the option of moving the whole settlement to the south bank, the Chartered Company's Administration narrowed the choice down to two possible sites on the north bank, both along the line of the railway - one that was 'close to the Falls and the river' (known as Imbault's Camp) and the other on the 'sand-belt some seven miles (11 km) north' (at Constitution Hill).

Without consultation with the settlers, Coryndon, the Company's Administrator, decided upon Constitution Hill, where the Government Station, Post Office and Court House had already been established, believing that a town *"so close to the Falls would be bound to mar the natural beauty of the area"* (Phillipson,1990).

The Old Drift community did not agree with his choice.

> *"The Old Drifters, however, were opposed to a site so far from the Falls, which they felt would deprive them of the profits of the tourist trade. They proposed instead that the town be situated at the camp of Imbault, the Bridge Engineer, which was on a well-drained site overlooking the river."* (Phillipson,1990)

Writing at the end of the following year, a new arrival on the north bank, Leopold Moore, summarised the settlers arguments against the site.

> *"Before Livingstone was inhabited, before even, it was surveyed, its political history began in the shape of a unanimous expression of popular dissatisfaction with the site selected... The inhabitants pointed out the distance separating the new site from the Falls; its inaccessibility to tourists and others; the distance*

The Old Drift settlement

from the water supply; and the absence of any industry or enterprise in the neighbourhood to justify its existence, in the event of its failing to become a resort for visitors. The danger of an opposition township springing up, in a more favourably situated position, on either the South or North bank was urged, and subsequently, the difficulty of constructing roads or of obtaining suitable foundations for brick building in the sandy soil." (Livingstone Mail, December 1906)

Whilst the Old Drifters were unhappy with the proposed relocation site, the days of the Drift were undoubtedly coming to a close.

"But the Nemesis that was to destroy the Old Drift was the railway and the railway bridge. No more would the drift be needed; all goods would be transported easily and efficiently by train. Time would be saved and several miles would be cut off the journey of the goods." (Watt, undated)

Birth of Livingstone Town

The Administration were unmoved by the arguments of the settlers and planning for the new town continued, with Mr Rudolf Cloete appointed as surveyor. In November 1904 Coisson visited the site of the proposed settlement.

"The roads have been surveyed, one sees little white flags which mark them through the bush. The railway is near by, all well levelled but without tracks, they will be laid as soon as the bridge over the Maramba will make it possible for the engine to cart the material over it. Next week the land on the township site will be sold in small square holdings. In the centre the price is £100 and the outskirts £50." (Baxter and Clay, 1964)

Despite plans to hold the auction in late 1904 the Chartered Company finally auctioned 100 stands to the highest bidders on 23rd February 1905 (Baxter and Clay, 1964). To avoid speculation purchasers had to agree to erect on their stands a building to the minimum value of £300 within twelve months.

"The date was widely publicised in the Bulawayo Chronicle and some people from Bulawayo ventured north. In fact thirty of the seventy attending the sale were from that town. The buyers stood on the Market Square (Barotse Centre) with the bush crowding in around them. The roads had been cleared and, therefore, defined the blocks, but the stands were left with their dense growth of trees and shrubs. Despite their antagonism to this position on the sand belt, one third of the Old Drifters, including L F Moore, who was one of the prime movers for Livingstone's site being more sensibly placed, bought stands in the new township." (Watt, undated)

Phillipson later recorded:

"The township itself was laid out as a rectangular gird of streets and sanitary lanes forming fifteen blocks, in all covering an area of rather less than one square kilometre. The central street, Mainway (now Mosi-oa-Tunya Road) was to be forty-three metres wide. The central block was to be an open park, known as the Barotse Centre, which still survives. The remaining fourteen blocks comprised two hundred and four stands. Some of these were reserved for the Administration's offices and others for Old Drift residents who were to be forced to abandon their old settlement." (Phillipson, 1990)

Auction day, Constitution Hill

Leopold Moore and The Livingstone Mail

Mr (later Sir) Leopold Frank Moore arrived on the banks of the Zambezi in 1904, setting up residence at the Old Drift before relocating to the new town of Livingstone, where he would become a central figure in the early development of the frontier town.

On arrival at the Old Drift Moore took up the vacant role of chemist. His predecessor, Mr Southurst, had wandered into the veld in a fit of malarial fever and been found dead soon after (Roberts, 2020a).

Moore founded the Livingstone Mail in March 1906, three months after William Trayner had officially launched the rather informal Livingstone Pioneer and Advertiser. Six months later Trayner published his final issue.

"Leopold Moore did not take kindly to the Pioneer and on 31st March 1906 he started a rival weekly newspaper, the Livingstone Mail. It was typewritten on wax stencils and produced on foolscrap duplicating paper in purple ink. While concentrating on local settler news and views it contained a modicum of international matter: the first issue included the winner of the 1906 Grand National, run seven days previously...

"The Livingstone Mail survived for sixty years and is a valuable source of information on the history of the town and country, particularly from the settler point of view. By May 1908 its circulation had risen to one hundred and seventy-five copies. In October of the previous year Moore had run into trouble: it was so hot that the wax on the duplicating stencils melted on the typewriter. Nothing daunted, he ordered a printing press which was installed in August 1908." (Phillipson, 1990)

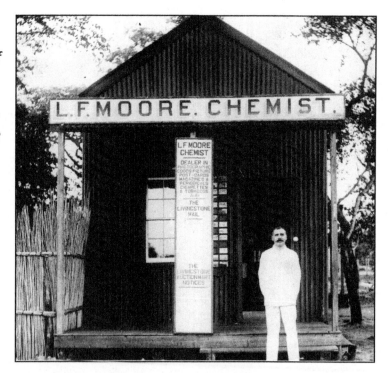

Moore outside his chemist shop, Livingstone

Livingstone on the Move?

Those who had invested in establishing the new town of Livingstone had high expectations of the development which would follow.

> "The prospect of the arrival of the railway provoked fantasies of economic growth, and global comparisons. It was confidently assumed that urban and industrial developments would be on the scale of Niagara City and Buffalo, which had grown up on the basis of power generated from the Niagara Falls... The South Africa Handbook of 1903 noted that thanks to the proximity of coal, minerals and water power, the site possessed 'all the factors for the creation of a great manufacturing centre. A new Chicago, let us call it Cecilton, will spring up near the banks of the Zambezi.' ... [In contrast] Niagara's precedent was invoked again in debates over conservation, this time offering a negative example. Lord Curzon was not alone in feeling that the Victoria Falls were more sublime than Niagara on the grounds of the 'lack of signs of civilization.'"
> (McGregor, 2009)

But industry, and tourism, was slow to reach Livingstone and residents in their dissatisfaction blamed the Chartered Company. Moore voiced his varied criticisms against the Company and its Administration through the pages of the Livingstone Mail, identifying the poor transport links between Livingstone and the Falls as a significant handicap to tourism.

> "Conductor Holland informs us that there were 101 passengers on board last Saturday's train de luxe. About a dozen of them managed to get as far as Livingstone. This is most unsatisfactory and it is to be hoped that some effort will be made... to provide transport facilities for our visitors." (Livingstone Mail, April 1906).

Mr Fred Mills opened the town's first significant Hotel, the Livingstone Hotel, in June 1906. Located on the corner of Queensway and Empire Street it was the first substantial brick building of any size and consisted of a bar, dining room and six bedrooms. A wagonette and six mules carried passengers to and from the station.

Mr Alfred L Lawley oversaw the construction of the town's second hotel for Pauling and Company (the railway construction contractors), the North-Western Hotel opening in July with Mr A B Stewart as manager.

> "The building, mainly of wood and iron, was built by Paulings the contractors on the construction of the Railway, as a hotel and was opened about July 1906.

Although at the time it was a better hotel than the one at the Falls, the poor communications between the Victoria Falls and Livingstone made it unattractive and it was a white elephant." (Woods, 1960)

By August 1906 rumours were in circulation concerning the ongoing campaign by the residents, led by Moore, to relocate Livingstone to a site closer to the Falls. A front-page headline from the Livingstone Mail in June 1907 claiming that the move had finally been approved turned out to be wishful thinking.

Under New Management

In August 1906 Henry Holland arrived to take up duties as the new Manager of the Hotel, having previously been the Conductor on the Train de Luxe. His new responsibilities included, as with his predecessor, overseeing the management of the railway's developing catering services. Before leaving the Hotel Mr Gavuzzi had in December 1905 also became manager of the Carlton Hotel, Johannesburg, and for a while regularly travelled between the two hotels, before eventually moving permanently to South Africa. Mr G Estran and Mr W Scott-Rodger, managers of the Falls Hotel and The Grand Hotel, Bulawayo, appear to have dissolved their partnership around the same time, with Mr W Scott-Rodger being identified in an advert as the sole proprietor of The Grand in September 1906 (Bulawayo Chronicle, September 1906).

Mr Holland faced a baptism of fire, with all of the Indian waiters working at the Hotel going on strike. Details of the cause of the strike are unknown, but they were promptly summoned before the local Justice of the Peace and fined.

> *"All the Indian waiters at the Falls Hotel went on strike on Tuesday afternoon. Next morning they appeared before the local J.P, Mr Fuller, and were given the option of paying a fine or going to durance vile; the fines were paid and the waiters left by Thursday's train for the South. The Hotel management promptly dealt with the difficulty and inspanned their... [management] staff to attend to the dinning-room; the improvement was noticed by all."* (Livingstone Mail, August 1906)

In addition to dissatisfied staff, Mr Holland also had to deal with the occasional unsatisfied customer:

> *"I have just worried through - I cannot say eaten - quite the beastliest meal I have faced since we left England. To do it justice it ought to stand out in one's memory as an occasion of great moral self restraint... Unfortunately this*

Mr Henry Holland

evening's performance is by the particular bandit who runs the Victoria Falls Hotel, so pray for us during the time we are under his domination: and, if I die, prosecute the ruffian. He is called Holland, is an ex-Railway Conductor, and is rapidly bringing the hotel to ruin." (Walker, 1907)

To top it all, the Hotel book-keeper accidentally shot himself in the arm whilst climbing in the gorge, as recorded in the Livingstone Mail:

"Mr Ward, book-keeper at the Victoria Falls Hotel, while scrambling down a precipitous portion of the gorge, about a mile and a quarter [2 km] from the Hotel, got entangled with his rifle which went off, blowing away a portion of the upper part of his left arm."

Mr Ward was rescued later that same day, securely strapped into a chair, his arm held firm in splints, and hauled up to safety by ropes.

"The greatest credit is due to all concerned for the plucky way in which they went to his assistance. We sincerely hope that an amputation will not be found necessary and that we shall soon see him amongst us again." (Livingstone Mail, October 1906)

A Final Visit

Mr (later Sir) Ralph Williams returned to the Falls a third and final time in August 1906, after reopening a route from the Okavango to the Falls via the Chobe, last used by the hunter Frederick Courtney Selous in 1878.

"We travelled down the Zambesi to Livingstone... and one morning walked up to the delightfully comfortable house of Mr Frank Sykes, the well-known Civil Commissioner, and for the first time since leaving Mafeking early in the previous May, experienced the pleasures of civilisation. From Livingstone I started on the same day to travel on a trolley to the Victoria Falls Hotel, but it broke down half-way, so with Mr Hodson I walked on, and on the 13th of August 1906 I once more walked over the famous Bridge, now entirely completed, and up to the

Victoria Falls Hotel, arriving there as grubby and as travel-stained as on my first visit to the same spot, then so wild and unknown, in 1883." (Williams, 1913)

Brighton on the Zambezi

A newspaper article from late 1906 promoted new developments at the Falls.

"The popularity of Victoria Falls, Rhodesia, as a winter resort for English men and women, is increasing to such an extent that it has been found necessary to augment the railway service and to increase the Hotel accommodation at the Falls. Mosi-oa-Tunya, as the natives call the new watering-place, had until quite recently only a temporary railway station, and an Hotel answering the same description. Now substantial structures have been substituted to form the nucleus of the future Brighton on the Zambesi.

"Cook's are receiving many inquiries regarding autumn and winter trips to the Falls. At present the cost of reaching there is quite discouraging to the cheap excursionist. The first-class return fare from London to the Falls amounts to £162 1s. 3d. The Hotel charges average about 22s. per day. Many fashionable people are going as far as Uganda, in order to escape the London fogs. A revolver and some skill in using it, should form part of the outfit taken on this tour." (Brisbane Telegraph, November 1906)

To Be or Not to Be?

In May 1905 members of the Livingstone community, still dissatisfied with the location of the new town, petitioned the Administration that the Falls Hotel be demolished, arguing that all tourists should be accommodated and served from Livingstone, as had been intended when the railway and town had been originally planned. They also contended that the (then still unpainted) Bridge was a *"red monster,"* to reach which *"an ugly gash had been scoured across the countryside"* (Rhodesia Railways Magazine, August 1955). The Hotel, and indeed Percy Clark, had even been granted trading licenses to run general stores and curio shops on the south bank, causing further consternation, especially when others tried and failed to obtain similar licenses.

The ongoing existence of the Hotel was a significant source of frustration for the Company's Administrator for North-Western Rhodesia. Coryndon supported the concerns of Livingstone residents and did his best to have the Hotel removed from its site, deploring the positioning of the buildings within sight of the Falls. The Livingstone Mail finally concluded early in 1907:

"[The Administrator] *announced that he had failed in his endeavours to have... [the Hotel] abolished. It had originally been erected as temporary accommodation for engineers, etc. employed on the Bridge and Railway construction, and for visitors to the Falls, and was to be pulled down as soon as a new township* [of Livingstone] *was laid out; He could hold out no hope of this being done, however.*" (Livingstone Mail, January 1907)

Livingstone became the capital of North-Western Rhodesia at the end of the same year, bringing at least some life to the struggling township. The town remained the capital after the formation of Northern Rhodesia in 1911 (following the amalgamation of the territories of North-Eastern and North-Western Rhodesia) up until 1935 when the administration was moved to Lusaka, the current capital.

With the relocation of the capital to Livingstone the Administration purchased the town's most significant building, the North-Western Hotel to become Government House. Within a few years a second, grander North-Western Hotel opened, managed by Fred Mills, also owner of the Livingstone Hotel. In March 1909 the Livingstone Mail carried a front page advert for the new Hotel:

"The North-Western Hotel (Proprietor F W Mills) will be opened on Thursday 1st April, Finest brands of liquors and cigars. Banquets and private dinners specially catered for. Special terms for month boarders... Carriages meet every train. Manager: Paul McUlenbergh, Late of Victoria Falls Hotel and Livingstone Club." (Livingstone Mail, March 1909)

Mr Holland's Last Hurrah

Mr Holland departed early in 1908, with a grand farewell banquet held at the Hotel in his honour on 1st February. A detailed sketch and description of the evening was printed in the Livingstone Mail (and reproduced in full in Creewel, 2004).

"On arrival at the Falls Hotel, we were shown to our respective rooms (the invitation included bed and breakfast) and afterwards made ourselves comfortable till dinner-time - eight o'clock. Punctually the gong was sounded and, without unnecessary delay, close on 40 sharp-set, well-seasoned pioneers trooped into the big dining-hall. The tables were laid in the form of a horseshoe, with genial host Holland in the centre chair. At the far end of the room, a scheme of decoration had been most tastefully carried out. It represented the Falls Bridge and the waterfall behind. The material used was coloured paper, and the structure spanned the platform."

Preparations for Mr Holland's leaving party

After dinner Leopold Moore, prime campaigner against the existence of the Hotel for many years, conducted the congratulations:

"A flashlight photograph was taken by Mr Percy Clark, and then business commenced... Mr Holland having proposed 'The King', and the toast having been duly honoured, Mr L F Moore rose to propose the toast of the evening...

"Mr Holland, your friends, seated around your hospitable board, have deputed me to speak for them on his happy occasion. They would wish me to say, I think, that they have all thoroughly enjoyed a most excellent dinner (cheers) and that their only feeling of regret is occasioned by the reflection that it is probably the last they shall have with you. Some of your friends present this evening have known you since you were a guard on the North-eastern Railway, many more, when you were the genial and popular conductor of the Train de Luxe, and all have known you as the most popular host the Victoria Falls Hotel has ever had, or for that matter, is ever likely to have (applause). I have no hesitation in saying that the Victoria Falls Hotel was never so well run as under Mr Holland's management (cheers).'" (Livingstone Mail, February 1908)

Mr Holland was then presented with a large silver salver, inscribed 'Presented to Henry Holland by his friends at Victoria Falls and Livingstone, on his departure, February 1st 1908.'

Railway Reorganisation

In late 1907 the Railway Company contracted the services of Mr C C Harvey, an American railway manager with wide experience *"to examine and report on the working of the entire system of railways."* Mr Harvey's report was presented to the Railway Company the following year and appears to have led to some significant changes, including the first steps towards the relocation of the railway's administrative and management headquarters from Umtali (now known as Mutare) to Bulawayo, and taking over the operation of the Victoria Falls Hotel, which had been leased to private management since opening in mid-1904.

"During his visit to Rhodesia Mr C C Harvey... reported on what further steps could be taken to develop additional traffic over the lines, made a very careful and exhaustive study of the railway system, its organisation, and possibilities... In accordance with Mr Harvey's recommendation, the headquarters of the traffic department had been moved from Umtali to Bulawayo. At the same time, a commercial agent had been appointed at Bulawayo whose special duty would consist in working up traffic in every possible direction. He would also have under his care the supervision of the Victoria Falls Hotel, which had now been taken over by the Railway Company." (Bulawayo Chronicle, July 1908b)

Mr Thomas A Mallet took over the management of the Hotel in early 1908, becoming the first Manager to be directly employed under the Railway Company. Mr Mallet appears to have excelled in the management of the catering facilities at the Hotel, including providing a notable banquet on the Congo border in December 1909, celebrating the arrival of the railway, over 500 miles (800 km) beyond the Victoria Falls (Roberts, 2021a).

In 1910 the decision was taken to relocate the Railway Company's remaining office and management services from Umtali to the more central location of Bulawayo. Management of the railway dining car services, together with responsibility for operating station refreshment rooms and management of the Railway's hotels, were all consolidated under the newly formed Catering Department, headed by Mr Mallet.

"About this time Thomas A Mallett, who was managing the Victoria Falls Hotel for the railways, was called upon to inaugurate a catering department to control dining-cars, refreshments-rooms and hotels. Initially the department was operated from Victoria Falls but this soon proved inconvenient and Mallet was found offices at Bulawayo." (Croxton, 1982)

Centre of the Social Scene

The Hotel soon became a focal point of the social scene for Livingstone residents, with regular weekend gatherings, dinner dances and occasional performances by visiting musical entertainers, touring theatre groups and travelling artists.

Easter 1908 was a full house, with the arrival of the Train de Luxe, and another larger contingent from Johannesburg for three nights, together with the regular contingent from Livingstone, who despite their long-standing dissatisfaction with the location of the Hotel, still supported it fully in their patronage.

In May 1908 the Hotel hosted Mr Frank Wheeler of the Wheeler-Edwardes Gaiety Company, with their performance of 'The Girls of Gottenburg' - promoted in the Livingstone Mail as *"the most popular comic opera ever produced"* - and the following evening 'The Merry Widow,' supported with full chorus and orchestra. Tickets were sold separately or together with return rail transport from Livingstone, and the shows received great support from the local community (Livingstone Mail, May 1908).

> *"The Wheeler-Edwardes Gaiety Company also visited the Falls, and gave two performances; 'The Girls of Gottenburg,' and 'The Merry Widow,' both of which were well attended by the local population, though on this occasion reserved seats were £1 each. The railway authorities ran a return train each night. This visit was an event to be marked with a white stone in our annals, and was in every way successful."* (Livingstone Mail, December 1908)

Canoes and clients at the Landing Stage

Clark's River Safaris

In 1908 Percy Clark imported nine Canadian canoes and a motorised launch, establishing his own river safari operation on the south bank a short distance above the Falls, and providing a welcome leisure excursion for Hotel guests.

"In 1908 I bought nine canoes from Canada, and also got a motor-launch. With these I started a boating business, and right from the start it was a good, money-making enterprise. All the bookings were made at the Hotel... and I paid the Hotel a percentage." (Clark, 1936)

In March 1911 Clark announced in the Livingstone Mail the arrival of a new, larger motorised launch, the Inyandiza, which he operated from the boathouse on the northern bank.

Rickshaw Wrangles

Clark claims to have brought the first rickshaws to the Falls - led by a young African guide and often followed by another to help push the rickshaw through the soft sands.

"I searched for another idea for the transport of visitors to various points of interest about the Falls, and I hit on the notion of rickshaws. I imported a few of those vehicles, the first to appear about the Falls, and they became very

Rickshaw ride

popular indeed. I made a charge of half a crown for two persons to go together by rickshaw to the Bridge or the Boathouse - a charge which I think was eminently reasonable."

Clark recalls that a few months after introducing the rickshaws, an official from the Railway Company approached him insisting he lower his price.

"A few months after my institution of this popular means of conveyance one of the higher officials of the railway turned up at the Falls, and he sent me a very peremptory notice requiring my immediate attendance upon him at the Hotel... The manager's office was an apartment about ten feet by eight [3 m by 2.4 m]. When I went along to see the high-and-mighty official at my own time it was into this cubby-hole that I was invited for the interview...

"'Mr Clark,' he said, 'I have sent for you regarding the rickshaws. Your prices are much too high. One shilling would be enough to charge either to the boats or to the bridge...'

"There was nothing, of course, to allay my annoyance in his tone, and I did not bother to hide my feelings. 'My price is half a crown,' I said, 'and what authority have you, in any case, for laying down the law to me?'

"'I have advertised the price as one shilling,' he blustered, 'and that is the price you are going to charge!'

"'I'll see you in Hades first,' said I. 'If you want to charge that price you had better buy the damned rickshaws!'

"'How much do you want for them?'

"I quoted a price, and he accepted it... I was satisfied, but the manager of the Hotel wasn't. He met me right afterwards and told me that I wouldn't have got that price out of him. I told him I knew that, but that the rickshaws were worth the money." (Clark, 1936)

The rickshaws proved hard work for the guides and uncomfortable for passengers, often becoming dragged down in the thick sand or jolted over rough ground. The Hotel also used several pony carts to convey guests around the Falls.

Landslide Washes Line Away

Originally the railway line ran round in front of the Falls Hotel, trains arriving at the Railway Station before turning on a special extension of track and then looping back round in front of the Hotel before passing on down to cross over the Bridge. In early 1909, a torrential rainstorm, during which seven inches of rain fell in five hours, eroded the sandy soils and created a substantial landslide, resulting in a section of the line in front of the Hotel becoming unstable.

The train arrives in front of the Hotel

"The heavy rains are not yet finished with in this territory. During Wednesday night and the early hours of Thursday last there was a tremendous downpour which has serious interfered with railway traffic. The train which should have left Livingstone for Bulawayo early on Thursday morning was unable to depart until five o'clock in the afternoon, owing to a bad washaway on the Southern bank of the Zambesi, near to the Victoria Falls Hotel. Owing to the heavy rains, in many places persons travelling through the country find the paths quite submerged and are compelled to wade through two or three feet [0.6-0.9 m] of water." (Bulawayo Chronicle, April 1909)

The line was soon after re-laid with trains passing straight through the Station, on a new section of track curving down to the Bridge.

Mr Mallet Makes His Mark

Holiday weekends have always been busy periods for the Hotel, and Easter 1909 was no exception, with special tourist trains and the regular Livingstone locals. Mr Piet Erasmus, a building contractor based in Livingstone recalled one of what must have been many entertaining incidents on such occasions:

"There were some memorable characters in the Livingstone of those days. One of them was Skipper Swanson. We were at the old Victoria Falls Hotel one day and Skipper, who had had a few drinks, took on a bet with someone else in the party that for a case of whisky he would climb the very tall, very thick flagstaff outside the hotel. The bet was forgotten until we heard shouts of 'Hi,' 'Hi!' coming from outside - and there was Skipper at the top of the pole." (Northern Rhodesia Journal, July 1959)

The local clientele were surprised, however, by a notice which appeared in the Livingstone Mail the following week, announcing that the price charged for dinner to non-residents would be increasing to five shillings per head. It can be assumed that there was an incident of sorts the previous weekend, as Moore comments:

> "Mr Mallet's advertisement well speaks for itself. We have heard some account of the provocation he received and feel, with regret, that his action is amply justified. The Falls Hotel becomes the temporary domicile of all the most distinguished people visiting South Africa, and to turn the place into a beer garden every Saturday afternoon would be the maddest policy possible."
> (Livingstone Mail, April 1909)

In the same month the Hotel received another Royal visitor, Crown Prince Albert of Belgium, which perhaps explains Mr Mallet's eagerness to raise the overall standards of the Hotel and the behaviour of his regular clientele.

Exceptional Opportunities

In October 1909 the Bulawayo Chronicle published the impressions of a visitor to the Falls, Mr Francis Masey, a professional architect from the south, who expressed disappointment at the lack of imagination shown in developing visitor facilities and 'appalling structure of tin sheds' which made up the Hotel.

> "Mr Masey referred to his trip to the Falls, and commented on the absence of initiative and imagination which was only too much evidence there. One was grateful, he said, at the railway achievement in bringing one of the wonders

Pre-World War One New Year's Eve celebration

of the world within reach of ordinary flesh and blood. At the Falls Hotel, the catering in all the circumstances was excellent, but there congratulation must cease. The appalling structure of tin sheds called in veriest satire a hotel, should be removed at the earliest moment.

"'There are,' he continued, 'exceptional opportunities of establishing there one of the hotels of the world. There is the natural beauty spot - probably the most wonderful on the face of the globe; there is unlimited power to supply light and water - and water is a magic fluid in South Africa; there is a climate warm and moist which will raise any sub-tropical fruit to perfection, and produce orchids and flowering shrubs in any variety; and there is a river on which it should be possible to arrange delightful excursions and, at a small cost, provide luxurious bathing facilities.'

"Mr Masey then proceeded to indicate the lines on which he would proceed to realise surroundings more in keeping with the demands of the scene. 'First of all I would build, not a hotel in the ordinary sense, but a series of small houses, each house, however, being so constructed that the rooms could be let separately and each provided with deep, cool stoeps or varandahs. They would be further away from the railway than is the present hotel, so that occupants should not be wakened during the night by passing and shunting goods trains. I would have a central building consisting of dining and billiard rooms, etc. The construction would be suitable to the place. It would be native in character. When one visits Paris one wants to see something essentially Parisian; when one visits the Victoria Falls one wants to see something characteristic of the country. For this reason I would have thick walls, plastered and whitewashed, Rhodesian asbestos ceilings, and thatched roofs, with deep overhanging eaves, with the large rooms fitted up with punkahs and the private ones with electric fans. I would have furniture of native timber, such as is made in Nyasaland, and mats, rugs and cushions all of native workmanship. I would have lawns for tennis and croquet leading off a spacious terrace, on which native bands could play, and I would certainly have a couple of large, fine swimming baths.'

"'I would,' said he in conclusion, 'also run a Victoria Falls season year, shutting down the hotel in the off-season as is done with some of the hotels in Egypt. I wouldn't have anything luxurious in the way of living. Everything of the 'fresh' variety should be produced on the estate so to speak - fruit, vegetables, milk, butter, eggs, meat. It should be good but simple. To my mind, something like what I have outlined is what Rhodes would have liked, and, moreover, had he been here he would have seen it done ere now.'" (Bulawayo Chronicle, October 1909)

The Weekender

From 1910 a special weekly passenger train service ran from Livingstone to Victoria Falls, known popularly as 'The Weekender' and transporting Livingstone socialites over the Bridge for Saturday night dances at the Falls Hotel.

"To meet the desires of the residents, a local train service was started and this was operated from about 1910 for many years on Saturdays and Sundays. The train usually consisted of one first-second class composite carriage and a good's guard's van hauled in the early days by one of the Nasmyth Wilson 4-4-0 tender locomotives and later by a 7th class 4-8-0. The train was colloquially known as The Weekender and the Saturday night dances at the Falls Hotel brought good patronage from the young people, especially as the railway detached one or two carriages at Victoria Falls station into which in the small hours the tired dancers would retire for a few hours rest before the carriages were coupled up to the northbound train back to Livingstone.

"For a time in 1916 the steam train was replaced by the first Rhodesian railcar. This 'rail motor coach,' as it was officially described, was propelled by a 70hp petrol engine; it was 24ft [7.3 m] in length and seated twenty passengers with a little space at one end for light packages. Built by the Drewry Car Co in England it did not remain in service for a very long." (Croxton, 1982)

The regular weekend service appears to have attracted an increasing number of entertainers to the Falls, including the return of Mr Wheeler and his company.

"In June commenced a remarkable series of public entertainments. Livingstone is not, normally, a very festive place, and during the previous two years only one company of entertainers had tempted fortune, with somewhat melancholy results. However, a concert party, the Wheeler-Edwardes Operatic Company, the Musical Madcaps, a quartete of famous operatic singers, including John Harrison of gramophone fame, the Edouin-Edwards Company and Mrs Chas Howitt with his full company all gave entertainments which on the whole were fairly well patronised, though it is to be feared that none would be considered commercial successes. The parties were visiting the Falls and endeavoured to make expenses. Anyhow, Livingstone was en fête and we believe thoroughly enjoyed itself." (Livingstone Mail, December 1910)

Reports of the evening's entertainment even appeared in the pages of the Bulawayo Chronicle.

The Weekender on the Bridge

"A large number of the inhabitants of Livingstone spent a very enjoyable evening at the Victoria Falls Hotel on Monday last when a costume recital was given by the Wheeler-Edwardes' Gaiety Company. The railway company ran a special train from Livingstone to the Falls. Livingstonians did not hesitate to avail themselves of this rare opportunity for an evening's diversion. 'Costume' recital seem rather a misnomer for an entertainment in which so few of the performers appeared in 'costume.' The programme was appreciated by the audience. With his usual hospitality Mr Mallet invited the visitors to partake of supper as his guests.

"Many persons were disappointed to find that the railway company had decided to start the special train from Livingstone Station and not from the town as was at first thought; and they were relieved to find on the return journey that the railway company were good enough to run the train as far as the town and thus save the tired passengers the somewhat lengthy journey from the station."
(Bulawayo Chronicle, June 1910)

Rail Connections

Special connecting train services were the life-blood of the Hotel, bringing cruise liner passengers from the Cape in the south and Beira on the east coast, often in groups of hundreds at a time. First class return trips from the Cape to the Falls took thirteen days - including four days spent at the Falls and three nights at the Hotel.

"Special excursions were organised... each trip lasting thirteen days. Tourists spent four days at the Falls and they were also shown the sights of Bulawayo, the Matopas, Mafeking and Kimberley. First class return fare from Cape Town, including all meals and bedding, was nineteen pounds ten shillings. Tourists were informed that eleven Union Castle mail steamers placed end to end would just reach across the Falls." (Green, 1968)

Following the formation of the Union of South Africa in 1910, cruise ship tourism to the Cape, and travel into the interior by train, was heavily promoted, with the Victoria Falls the jewel in Africa's crown. A 1911 South African Railway pamphlet promoted the Falls as *"the most beautiful gem of the earth's scenery"* (Green, 1968). In 1913 there were five special excursion trains from the Cape alone.

Difficult Customers

One early railway traveller to the Falls was Mrs Getcliffe, of Cheshire, England, who travelled on a special train service from Johannesburg and wrote of her travels in the 'Macclesfield Courier & Herald' in 1910. The train carried 100 passengers, 20 staff, two dining cars, a food supply wagon and five tons of ice.

"There were three passengers in each compartment, the remaining berth being used for our luggage. The seats were very comfortable, being fitted with springs, and at night they were turned into beds with pillows, sheets, etc. Each compartment had a lavatory basin and a looking glass so that passengers could either dress in their compartments or, if they so preferred, in the bathrooms."

Mrs Getcliffe and her companion stayed at the Hotel and recorded:

"We were not charmed with the accommodation or the service, but when we felt inclined to complain we reflected that all the food had to be brought from Cape Town or Beira, and that there are no shops nearer than Bulawayo, which is a 20 hours journey by rail."

Crossing the Bridge to visit the town of Livingstone Mrs Getcliffe appears to have again been unimpressed:

"One day we visited the town of Livingstone, a few miles north of the Falls. It is difficult to imagine how people live there in the great heat, and what they do for a living. There are few shops... about four blocks of houses and a club. To be Chief Magistrate and His Majesty's Representative in such a place is certainly paying the penalty of greatness." (Rhodesia Railways Magazine, March 1962)

Good Vibrations

Mr William Agate and his party arrived in the Falls in mid-1910, staying in the Annex buildings:

"Really four semi-detached bungalows (much frequented by honeymoon couples we were told); two of which were taken for our use, and were found to be most comfortable... Everything was really very nice at the Hotel, except the large quantities of Zambesi hornets, which seemed to take a special fancy to our bedrooms...

"There are also great troops of baboons... one biggish fellow had the audacity to seat himself on the tennis-court of the Hotel, and was promptly shot by the manager, but only wounded. The brute made a dreadful jammer, and his chums came out of the bush and carried him away, but not before they had tried to extract the bullet. The manager told me that the scene was so human, he was sure he could never bring himself to fire again at a baboon."

With the Falls in full flood, Agate records the ground vibrations caused by the huge volume of falling water:

"One seems to feel a distant tremor in the earth beneath one's feet... more perceptible when lying in bed at night. It was also distinctly queer to hear the window casements in our bungalow rattling on a windless night."

Agate refers to rumours of a grand five-storey building planned for the site.

The Hotel Annexes

"A hundred yards away from our halting place today, is the site of the Victoria Falls Hotel which may be built next year, and according to the published plan is to be a delightful five-story building with ample verandas from which grand views of the Falls can be obtained." (Agate, 1912)

Corporate Team-building

A notable special private train service was arranged from Bulawayo in April 1911 when the management of the well-known Bulawayo department store, Haddon & Sly (established in 1894), took the entire personnel of the firm and their families to the Falls for the Easter break, booking a private train and taking over the whole Hotel. Their adventure began on the way up, when the dining car jumped the rails.

"It was at breakfast the next morning (Good Friday) that we had our first and, happily, the only really exciting experience. The dining car was full of people having breakfast when all of a sudden there was a series of bumps, and before we really knew what had happened the car tilted and all our breakfast cups and saucers and plates were jolted on to the floor... We were extremely fortunate in having our breakdown opposite a railway ganger and his boys, and it was due to their energies, the help of the staff of a goods train which caught us, and our own guard and staff that we got righted in the time we did. Had the mishap taken place on a straight we would have only been delayed twenty minutes, but as it was on a curve we were delayed for five hours."

The party numbered over a hundred people, more than the Hotel could accommodate.

"As our party was such a large one it was only possible for the ladies to have rooms at the Hotel, the gentlemen having to sleep on the train. Mr Mallet did everything he could to make us comfortable and the success of our stay was largely due to his efforts. After an excellent dinner most of us went off to see the Falls by moonlight. It was a glorious night and the wonderful sight enchanted us." (Rhodesia Railways Magazine, April 1955a)

A Tricky Situation

The writer Olive Schreiner visited the Falls in June 1911, arriving by train and staying at the Hotel, succinctly described by her travelling companion Gregg:

"The food was quite good, whisky an exorbitant price, and a drink of water hard to obtain, whilst the world's greatest Falls thundered loudly near-by."

Hotel pony-carts (donkey-led rickshaws)

After exploring the surroundings of the Falls, Schreiner and her party undertook an eventful cruise to explore the islands on the river above the Falls:

"We were nearly all drowned on Wednesday. The motor boat we were in broke down and we were drifting down on to the Falls. We were only saved by a canoe coming past and going for help to the landing and calling six more canoes which took us all out and towed the boat to land. The pluck of all the women and girls except one miserable old Christian was wonderful... The curious thing is that having been so near death in its arms instead of making me feel horror of it, seems to draw me so much nearer it - my Falls that I was nearly part of!!" (Walters and Fogg, 2007)

In later years a floating boom was installed just below the landing stage across to a nearby island to catch any boats experiencing such engine trouble.

Critical Comments

The travel writer Catherine Cameron visited the Falls as part of her round Africa tour, travelling by train from Beira and publishing her travelogue in 1913. Cameron records staying at the Hotel and having quite an adventure exploring the Falls (somehow getting lost on her way to the Rainforest). The next day she took a rickshaw ride and canoe trip to Livingstone Island, seeing the initials of David Livingstone carved onto the now famous tree.

"A guide accompanies me. Victoria Falls Hotel has an inadequate supply of conveyances - only one guide, two rickshaws, and several old carts. One can imagine with twenty-five guests, each clamouring for attendants, the

disadvantages of sight-seeing. If only the Hotel management, after enticing you by splendid advertisements to cross Africa, would deign to provide better comfort for their guests, all would be well. There is no more beautiful scenery in the world. The property belongs to the Chartered Company. This Hotel is old-fashioned, and should be rebuilt. However, it has the monopoly, and refuses to modernize, nor will it allow its land to be sold. An enterprising American desired to purchase real estate and erect an enormous hotel costing a million dollars; but his schemes were foiled. The Victoria Falls Hotel consists of a collection of primitive corrugated-iron houses, bungalow style, walls inside being of rough boards. There are a verandah and annexes which rest on wooden piles, but the whole edifice shakes as you walk.

"What they need is a fine three-storeyed building facing the Falls, where the view would prove magnificent. I presume the authorities' philosophy is, 'We have the eighth wonder of the world. If you want to see it you must pay our prices and put up with accommodation offered.' I paid 21s. a day pension... The bedroom I occupied could not be styled pretty or comfortable. The iron bedstead held a thin mattress which reminded me of a sandwich. Every time one turned the wires groaned dreadfully, and two of the hardest and smallest pillows completed the discomfort. A precocious green window-blind would not go up or remain down, but chose its own level, while the matchboard walls were a sickly green. An early Victorian mirror with a side broken enabled you to dress, and in the corner a wooden triangle, supporting a blue rag, served as a wardrobe. The dining-room was commodious and food quite all right.

"It was very amusing next morning, since all the guests had gone through the same experience as myself. Their clothes and boots were taken... [by room

The creeper-covered verandah

service] *to be dried... Between seven and eight a dozen heads bobbed out of doors, crying, 'Boy, I want my clothes - my boots!'"* (Cameron, 1913)

A 1913 Hotel advert promoted the Hotel's location *"situated within ten minutes of the most magnificent and stupendous scene on the face of the earth... Words cannot picture the majestic beauty of the Victoria Falls."* The Hotel itself claimed to be *"the most modern hotel in Rhodesia,"* boasting, among other luxuries, *"cuisine par excellence, ...hot and cold shower baths"* and *"perfect sanitation."* Supporting images of the Hotel show the front verandah now enveloped by creepers, presumably offering some welcome shade, and the Hotel's 'pony-traps' (donkey-led rickshaws) used to transport guests to various locations around the Falls, whilst promising *"comfortable motor launches and safe Canadian canoes are to be had at all times"* (Victoria Falls Hotel, 1913).

A Tropical Fairyland

Another rail visitor to the Falls and guest at the Hotel, Ms Amy V Fuller, arrived in late 1914. Ms Fuller recorded a detailed description of her visit.

> *"There is no town of Victoria Falls the nearest village being that of Livingstone, a few miles further up the line; but behind the station there is the hotel run by the railway department, and a few thatched kraals belonging to the curio traders-and scattered about one comes upon a few native huts from time to time. The Hotel tariff is £1 1s. a day and they say even so it does not pay. The building is low and rambling, chiefly corrugated iron, painted red - and the heat is intense through the day - the thermometer registering as much as 106 deg.* [Fahrenheit, 41 degrees Celsius] *in the entrance hall. The bedrooms are decidedly small and common place - such as one would expect at a very indifferent hotel - but they have added a fine large dining room, where Indian waiters with their turbans and white costumes give one quite a feeling that one is in India. The plans are now fixed for a large building, which will be commenced as soon as the season is off.*
>
> *"Instead of leaving the train at the Falls station, we handed our baggage over to the hotel servants, and went on over the Bridge. A charge of 1s. return is made for foot passengers crossing the bridge to the next station, which is Palm Grove. Early morning, everything wet with night showers, and a tropical feeling in the air, was what greeted us when we left the railway siding, and we wandered beside the mighty Zambesi, simply entranced. It seemed a fairyland - so fresh and green, palms and tropical trees and flowers, papyrus, etc., on all sides."*
> (Perth Western Mail, February 1915)

The Hotel Rebuilt

By 1912 plans for the long overdue redevelopment of the Hotel were well advanced. Having secured the future of the Hotel on the site, the Railway Company now finally planned to erect permanent brick buildings. Preliminary drawings were supplied by Sir Charles Metcalfe, but the final designs, dated April 1912, were executed in Bulawayo by architect Frank Scott.

"Sketch plans exist showing a number of proposed designs - from a simple, long-bungalow type building to a grand, two-storey design, with a balcony facing the Falls. The common feature was the spaciousness of the rooms and the high ceilings to keep the interior cool." (Creewel, 2004)

Mr Charles Corner, Resident Engineer for the Railway Company based in Bulawayo, appears to have worked with Sir Charles on the plans for the new Hotel buildings. A copy of the plan for the 'Proposed Hotel, Victoria Falls' in Mr Corner's photographic album is annotated by hand *"Grand Plans by Sir C Metcalfe & C.C."* (Corner, undated). Mr Corner was responsible for the design of the railway buildings at Gwelo (now Gweru), including the Station Master's house (both built in 1902), and the General Manager's house and new station at Bulawayo (built 1911 and 1913 respectively). Mr Corner also served as Acting General Manager during the opening of the railway line to the Congo border in 1909 (Roberts, 2021a).

Livingstone based brick-maker and builder Piet Erasmus was one of many contractors who were involved in the work (Northern Rhodesia Journal, July 1959).

Construction work begins

The Victoria Falls Hotel, Ltd

The Victoria Falls Hotel Company was formed by the Railway Company in 1914 to raise the capital investment necessary to fund the building and equipping of the new Hotel and to manage the Hotel's buildings, assets and investments. The Company also had provision to *"institute a service of tugs and boats on the Zambezi River; ...and to carry on the business of pleasure boating"* (Victoria Falls Hotel Ltd, 1914).

The nominal capital raised was £50,000, divided into one-pound shares, the major shareholders initially being the Beit Trust. Later share issues would result in the Railway Company taking over the larger share of the Company. The Hotel Company negotiated the lease of an extended plot of land on which the Hotel was built from the 1st January, 1914, for a period of 51 years, with a token annual payment of £5, paid half to the Railway Company and half to the Chartered Company. The Hotel occupied two legal plots of land - the original 9.83 acres within the Victoria Falls Station Railway Reserve and an adjoining 7.36 acres of Railway Reserve. There was a further agreement whereby the Victoria Falls Hotel Company leased the operational management of the Hotel back to the Railway Company, for a period of 50 years from 1st January 1915 (Victoria Falls Hotel Ltd, 1919).

Built in Brick

The new buildings were constructed from 1914, with the work delayed by the impacts of the First World War. Furnishing and fitting of the buildings further delayed the opening of the new Hotel until mid-1917, at an approximate construction cost of £40,000, although it is likely that works continued into the following year.

View of new Hotel showing viewing towers

The Hotel Entrance

"According to an advertisement in the Rhodesia Journal of 1916/17, the new hotel was due to open on April 1st 1917 but, in that month, the Livingstone Mail reflected that; 'Furnishing of the new hotel at the Falls is coming on.' It is probable that the hotel opened sometime in June of that year." (Creewel, 2004)

The cool and spacious single-storey structure, consisting of a central building and two flanking side wings giving views over the gorge and rising spray of the Falls, housed twenty-four bedrooms and two private suites. Bathroom facilities were provided in each wing and the baths themselves were remembered for their vast size - they were so deep that children were not permitted to use them unaccompanied.

"The walls were massive - nine inches solid - and provided 24 bedrooms, two suites and five public rooms: the lounge; writing room; drawing and music room; smoking room and dining room. There was also a small private bar and office accommodation to the left and right of the main entrance. Lest it be forgotten, there had to be supporting services - electricity was provided by a private company, but considerable plant was required to provide water and refrigeration." (Creewel, 2004)

The spacious new Dining Room was designed with echoes of features from the original railway shed which had served as the Hotel's first dining room, an example being the high oval windows, also a feature of the Lounge. Another short wing housed the Hotel's kitchens. Guests could relax in the Lounge, find time for

quiet reflection in the Writing Room, or socialise in the Drawing and Music Room, Smoking Room or small private bar. The furniture was imported from Waring & Gillow, England, and one of the additional facilities provided at the Hotel was a darkroom for the use of amateur photographers. Office administration and services were located to the left and right of the Reception Hall. Two viewing towers, either side of the main wing, gave views over the gorges to the Bridge and Falls.
The Hotel laundry was steam operated from the customised boiler of a Kitson-Meyers railway engine, decommissioned in 1912 after service at Hwange Colliery, and which remained on site and operational for over eighty years.

The British South Africa Annual for 1916-7 included a detailed description of the new Hotel buildings (and reproduced in full in Creewel, 2004).

"The building is a long single-storey structure, with two flanking bedroom wings set out at swinging angles on each side. The... building is planned on spacious lines suitable for the much larger bedroom accommodation which will follow when the future second story is added. The two main features in the way of staterooms are the lounge and dining room, both handsome, spacious rooms treated in a suitable architectural manner. The building is of fireproof construction, its framework and roof being of reinforced concrete; the outer walls being filled in with brickwork from floor level to roof level. The roof is perfectly flat in concrete, with a protective covering of bitumastic sheeting. It is reached by two imposing staircases and forms a roof garden from which charming views of the gorge, bridge and surrounding country can be obtained.

"The building is approached on the west front from the railway station through a vaulted vestibule leading direct into the lounge, from which corridors branch off

The front of the new Hotel

on either side to the extremities of the building. Passing across the lounge, the main loggia (a pillared stoep) is reached, and on either side of this are smaller loggias of lower height and lesser width. The eastern front is the main façade of the building and is approached from the loggia by a tier of steps running the full length of this feature. The building is cool, spacious and airy everywhere and, architecturally, is treated in quiet Southern European Renaissance manner. The exterior walls are coloured a light, cool cream, and this colour scheme has been generally carried out in the interior of the building.

"The Rhodesia Railways are to be congratulated on their enterprise, and I have no doubt that the extension of the building provided for in construction will be accomplished at no very distant date." (British South Africa Annual, 1916-7)

The old Annex buildings were decommissioned and removed from the site to make way for the new buildings. Photographs show the old main building situated alongside the new buildings, suggesting that the Hotel remained open and operating throughout the extended building period. It remained on site for several decades, serving to accommodate overflow during the busy season.

The focal element of the new Hotel was the columned veranda, with views of the gorge, Bridge and rising spray from the Falls. A special feature was a mosaic compass which was incorporated into the floor.

The Hotel Lounge

One of a handful of guests in the old Hotel buildings in December 1916 recalled how the Manager cleared a corner in the new Dining Room and served Christmas dinner. This was recorded as the first meal served in the Hotel's current Dining Room, much extended and rebuilt since, and now known as the Livingstone Room (Rhodesia Railways Magazine, December 1954). Advertisements for the new Hotel boasted *"every modern comfort"* and *"cuisine par excellence"* with *"the finest wines, spirits and cigars on hand."*

Global Influenza Pandemic

The global influenza pandemic of 1918-20, known as Spanish flu or the 'forgotten pandemic,' infected an estimated 500 million people across the world, from isolated Pacific islands to the remote Arctic fringes, claiming over 50 million lives - more than the number lost in the First World War and making it one of the deadliest natural disasters in recent human history. The pandemic reached Southern Rhodesia in October 1918, affecting the whole country, particularly the high-density mining communities.

> *"The epidemic spread like wildfire through the country, treating white and black folk alike, taking toll of all. Victoria Falls suffered with the other towns and settlements, For a fortnight not one train arrived from Bulawayo, there being neither engine-drivers nor firemen to man the engines. We were isolated from the rest of the world. No provisions or vegetables came in from the south... At the Falls we had scarcely one well person. At the Hotel, for example, the only person afoot of visitors and staff was the housekeeper. I was the only one in our household who was not down with the malady, and the sick included all our native servants, so that I had to look after all the invalids myself... At one time my wife and younger son were not expected to live...*
>
> *"When the epidemic was at its worst I had a visit from the Hotel housekeeper. She came to me with the request that I would make chicken broth for the visitors and staff of the Hotel who were down with flu. The request struck me as being a little thick, for the Hotel had a big kitchen and one or two boys about on their feet, while I had my hands full as it was, with not a soul to help me. Still, I saw a funny side to the request, and the laugh did me good. I told the lady that if she would have the chickens sent over I would do the rest."* (Clark, 1936)

In June 1919 the famous English singer and actress (and later Dame) Marie Tempest and her company stayed at the Hotel on their tour of South Africa, during which Ms Tempest gave an impromptu performance from Faust in the Lounge (Green, 1968).

On the River

The growth of Percy Clark's boating business on the river above the Falls had not gone unnoticed by the Falls Hotel. Recognising the potential profits if managed 'in-house' the General Manager of the Railway Company, Colonel Birney, eventually made Clark an offer for his boating business.

"As I refused to sell, the Hotel bought a launch for itself. This cooked my goose, for... all the bookings were made at the Hotel office. I had about as much chance of carrying on in opposition as I would have of coughing effectually against thunder." (Clark, 1936)

The Hotel purchased the launch boat 'Diana', named after the daughter of the railway's General Manager, Colonel Birney, and carrying up to 30 passengers. Two huts and a boat shelter were developed on the river at the launch site, a short distance upstream of the Falls. The Hotel also invested in four canoes and, oddly, 13 paddles. The launch trips operated upstream to Kandahar Island, where passengers would alight for a picnic, and the canoes ran downstream to Cataract Island, on the very lip of the Falls. Later, in 1928, the Hotel invested in a second launch, the 'Daphne', carrying up to 35, and soon after a third, the 'Dorothy,' carrying 10 passengers. A launchway was developed at the landing stage in 1928, and shelters built for the launches in 1938.

The Hotel's boat and canoe service was under the supervision of Mr Victor B Pare, who appears to have had more than just the occasional close shave with the local river hazard - the hippopotamus.

"Soon after World War I, the Victoria Falls Hotel launch set out full of visitors and a vindictive hippo appeared. It made an unprovoked rush for the boat, tore a piece from the stern, dived underneath and holed the boat amidships. Mr Pare was injured but the boat reached the river bank without sinking." (Green, 1968)

On the river

Trolley Transport

Always on the look out for a new business opportunity, Percy Clark claimed to have been the first to see the potential of a local rail transport system to take tourists from the Hotel to the Falls, Bridge and river:

"I now got another idea of making money, and I took a trip home on the strength of it. My notion was to run a trolley-line down to the Bridge and the landing-stage. I was very kindly received by the B.S.A.C. office in London, ...but after exhibiting details of my scheme I was told that the whole thing was in the province of the railway company... Then years went by, however, before the trolley-line came into being. I have always believed that I got the idea first, and believing that I think I ought to have shared the profit." (Clark, 1936)

The local rail trolley system was finally developed in 1920 by the Railway Company, at a cost of £4,000, and operated by the Hotel. A two foot gauge rail track was laid, running from close to the northern hammerhead wing of the Hotel directly down to the Falls, with separate spurs on to the Bridge and up along the river to the riverside landing stage where tourists could take river cruises.

"The trolley system had three sections, not physically connected. From the hotel, a double track ran one mile northward to 'Trolley Junction,' where passengers changed to two single track lines leading to the various points of interest. One line (the longest) ran eastward beside the Rain Forest to the Victoria Falls Bridge, and was later paralleled by a road; the other ran northward to the Landing Stage and Boat House, passing the Devil's Cataract... From the terminus of this line, three-quarters of a mile upstream from the Falls, tourists could join launch or canoe trips to the islands in the river. Photographs show two types of vehicle, a four-

Trolley tours

seat trolley with cross seats pushed by two Africans, and a knifeboard eight-seat trolley pushed by three or four. Each trolley had a roof and canvas awning, and a screw handbrake applied from either end." (Price, 1966)

Telephone boxes were installed at each terminus and junction so that a trolley could be summoned when required. The fare was one shilling per trip. The trolleys were available during the hours of daylight only, although special arrangements could be made with the Hotel Manager for night-time trips to see the lunar rainbow. The service was under the supervision of Mr Pare.

A Grave Matter

George Graves, a famous London West End actor and entertainer of the time, visited the Falls in 1922. He suffered an injury to a finger when the trolley on which he was travelling accidentally de-railed, resulting in a compensation claim for £1,500 being met the following year - effectively wiping out the operational profit of the Hotel for the year.

Despite his claim being successful it appears Mr Graves was at least partly to blame for the accident - as later described by a Livingstone resident.

"George Graves, the comedian, visited the Falls and was to give a show in Livingstone. The day of the show he and his party were on a trolley on which the visitors travelled from the Hotel to the Bridge. These trolleys were in charge of an African, as the gradient to the Falls was downhill all the way, but George Graves on this occasion dispensed with the native who was in charge and the party went off on their own. Soon the trolley began to gain speed and by the time it had nearly reached the end of the line, Graves did not brake early enough and consequently the trolley and party landed up on a sandbank at the end of the line. George Graves managed somehow to get his hand in the mechanism of the trolley and he had the top of his second finger taken off. He was taken to Livingstone Hospital and Dr Ellacombe operated and fixed the finger up.

"That evening, against doctor's orders, he appeared on the stage in a dressing gown and apologised for not being able to do his usual turn, but he told some funny stories and the rest of the company carried on with their part of the show. On his return to England it was reported in the Press that he had had the top of his finger taken off by a crocodile when he held his hand over the side of the canoe on a trip from the Falls to Kandahar Island." (Northern Rhodesia Journal, 1959)

A Visit from the 'Queen of Crime'

Agatha Christie, the 'Queen of Crime' and murder mystery fiction writing, stayed at the Hotel during a tour of southern Africa in March 1922, accompanied her first husband, Archibald Christie. She based her third novel, 'The Man in the Brown Suit' (1924) on her travels, the climax of which finds her leading characters at the Falls Hotel. In a letter to her mother, Christie wrote:

"It has been lovely here. I can't bear to leave. It's not just the Falls themselves, although they are very wonderful... but the whole place. No road, only paths, just the hotel and primeval woods for miles and miles stretching into blueness. A delightful hotel, long and low and white, with beautifully clean rooms, and wired all over like a fine meat safe against malarial mosquitoes."

Of the Falls she wrote:

"Great trees, soft mists of rain, its rainbow colouring, wandering through the forest with Archie, and every now and then the rainbow mist parting to show you for one tantalising second the Falls in all their glory pouring down. Yes, I put that as one of my seven wonders of the world." (Prichard, 2013)

Creewel records of Christie's visit:

"Mr Pare, had the honour of escorting her around. He no doubt presented her with a small animal carved from vegetable ivory, a local souvenir for which he was well known locally, and it has been suggested that he may be the person on whom she based the character of Harry Rayburn, who appeared in one of her later novels." (Creewel, 2004)

By the river

A Mysterious Monster

In 1925 Mr Fred Law, special correspondent with the London Daily Express, recorded the incredible story, sadly undated, of two visitors to the Falls.

"One day two Englishmen, spending a holiday in the region of the Victoria Falls, Rhodesia, appeared in the Hotel at dinner time with a tale of an extraordinary monster that had its home underneath the fall. It was rather like a huge serpent, pale in color, with a glossy skin texture. It swam like a gigantic eel, apparently quite at home in the seismic convulsions of the Boiling Pot, the name given to the granite basin which receives the whole thunder of the cataract.

"'How large was the monster?' They could not be sure; certainly, they never expected it to be believed, but one would imagine it to be fifty feet [15.2m] long and not all of it had been exposed. Perhaps, not half. After it had swum about vaguely for a time, as if seeking for something, it had disappeared without warning, and although they waited an hour it did not rise again. No one believed in the tale, of course. At the same time, numbers of people were seen to loiter near the vicinity during the next few days, gazing earnestly four hundred feet [122m] down into the swirling mysteries of the Boiling Pot. It was the dry season; there was little spray, and they had a clear view. But they saw nothing. The strange denizen of the place was silent, absent. Gradually his supposed existence was forgotten."

The article then goes on to report a more recent sighting of the creature, this time witnessed by Mr Pare and two guests at the Hotel.

"Years afterwards, a man, employed to take tourists for launch rides on the Zambesi and two women, tourists at the Hotel, were standing above the Falls at noonday. Suddenly the creature appeared. This time it had a head, or, rather, it was all head, all that could be seen of it. The head was estimated to be fifteen feet [4.5m] in length. As before, the monster swam about, as if at home, and vanished as it had appeared, without commotion." (Adelaide Chronicle, August 1925)

From Far and Wide

At the end of 1922 the Chartered Company and British Government began negotiations over the future of the Rhodesias following the end of the period of the Royal Charter. Southern Rhodesia was granted self-governing status in 1923 and Northern Rhodesia became a British Protectorate in 1924.

The Hotel was establishing a world-wide reputation for its high standards, quality service and of course, spectacular location. Global transport brought fine cuisine from far and wide to the Falls, with the Hotel menu offering the finest products and ingredients from across the world. The South African travel writer Green recorded:

"Memorable dishes were carried into the Victoria Falls Hotel dining-room during the gay 'twenties and afterwards; pâté de foie gras all the way from Strasbourg; smoked salmon from Scotland; lobsters and crawfish; all the classic items of charcuterie from raw Parma ham to Italian mortadella; mushrooms and truffles; grouse and quail and larger game birds decorated with their own plumage. The grand viziers of the kitchen sent in baskets of flowers made of spun sugar and masterpieces of marzipan. A special chef presided over a celebrated fish and cold meat buffet in the dining-room." (Green, 1968)

A growing North American market developed with the launch of round-the-world cruises, such as the 96-day 'Great African Cruise' undertaken from New York in 1926, including stops in South America, South Africa and Europe.

"Efforts were being made to foster the tourist trade and in 1926, in conjunction with the S.A.R. [South African Railways], two special trains carrying 350 American tourists from a world-cruise liner included visits to Bulawayo and Victoria Falls, the parties staying at the Falls Hotel for a couple of nights. The success of this tour, to be the forerunner of many more, led to the enlarging of the Hotel. Another fifty bedrooms were built, with bathrooms and other facilities, along with modern station offices in a style to harmonise with the Hotel." (Croxton, 1982)

Afternoon tea on the veranda, with mosaic compass design just showing on floor

The Hotel Extended

The Hotel's new Manager, Mr Tim Ward, who took over operations in 1923, oversaw the next expansion phase of the Hotel. The designs were drawn up by Mr J R Hobson, the Railway Company architect, who took great care to ensure the extensions were in keeping with the general style and design of the existing buildings, and the work undertaken by a Bulawayo construction firm.

Originally it was planned to create a second storey over the existing main building and wings, but this raised many structural problems. The alternative chosen was to extend the Hotel with the addition of two double-storey blocks at the end of each of the side wings, creating the famous 'hammerheads.' Hotel company reports show that £66,000 was raised from the issue of new shares.

The Hotel's kitchens were enlarged and the Dining Room extended by removing the end wall and lengthening the room to measure 100ft in length by 30ft (30.5 by 9.1 metres) and with capacity for over 200 seated diners and between 400 and 500 standing guests for special events.

Hammerheads and Summer Parlour

The two hammerhead extensions were built in 1926, greatly increasing the capacity of the Hotel with an additional 25 rooms in each block, including four private suites. Many of the new rooms came with private bathroom and toilet. To maintain the architectural axis and symmetry of the buildings, a second floor

Extension works in progress. Note the original Hotel building (centre right)

was added above the central Lounge rooms. The Summer Parlour, overlooking the gorge, Bridge and Falls, gave additional lounge space and became a popular meeting point for cocktails and sundowners.

Summer Parlour viewed from the front of the Hotel

Swimming Pool

In 1928 the swimming pool was opened, measuring 60ft by 30ft (18.2 by 9.1 metres) with a fountain constantly keeping the water moving. The pool was shielded from the Hotel by the changing rooms and surrounded by walls for privacy, but for many years there was no mixed swimming. This was reportedly as a result of a request by a visiting maharajah who wanted to swim, but not in view of female swimmers, and the instruction was apparently not withdrawn for some time. A citrus orchard, with oranges, lemons, naartjes and grapefruit, was established beyond the swimming pool area and maintained for several decades.

The Hotel Swimming Pool

Reception Hall

Court and Western Wings

The connecting Court Wing, on the northern side of the Hotel, and Western Wing, housing a new Reception Hall, were built in 1929. The additions extended the original plan of the Hotel with an axial line leading the visitor through the new Main Entrance and Reception Hall across the now enclosed Courtyard and middle of the old Hotel wing to the veranda and view of the gorge and Bridge beyond. When the Hotel is approached from the Railway Station a perspective view can be obtained from outside the Main Entrance, through both wings to the view beyond.

The new Main Entrance to the Hotel

Palm Courtyard

Along with the construction of the Court and Western wings, the now enclosed courtyard gardens were formally developed, with fountains playing into three ornamental ponds surrounded by green grass and paths of flagstones, quarried from an area called Pasipas outside Bulawayo.

"At one end of the Palm Court an historic tablet mounted upon a Pasipas stone pedestal gives information regarding the ancient history of the Victoria Falls, while at the other end a sundial specially designed for the tropics will record the time of day whether the sun is north or south of the Equator" (Rhodesia Railways Bulletin, May 1931).

Populations of aquatic mosquito larvae are controlled by local fish species which have been introduced and thrive in the ponds. Frogs and toads found their own way into the ponds, their nocturnal calls causing problems for some guests, and for a period the Hotel even employed a frog catcher to ensure guests had a good, and hopefully quiet, night's sleep (Caterer & Hotelkeeper Magazine, 1984).

Mr Ward is often credited for the planting of the many mango trees found in the Hotel grounds, although the family recall they were planted by his wife, Francesca (Ward, 2016). These now provide welcome shade, although the fruit are a seasonal attraction for baboons and also fruit bats, who add their distinctive calls to the nocturnal chorus.

The Hotel Courtyard

Hotel Chapel

A special feature of the Western Wing was the inclusion of the Chapel of Saint Mary Magdalene, consecrated on 28th February 1932 by the Right Reverend Edward Frances Paget, the Bishop of Southern Rhodesia and later Archbishop of Central Africa. The Chapel was provided for the use of the Railway Chaplain who toured the rail network giving services to employees. The Railway General Manager, Colonel Birney, felt the Chapel would be a source of great comfort for people working as well as staying at the Hotel.

Although the Chapel is officially an Anglican place of worship, members of many Christian faiths attend the services. The alter and dais are made of Indian Teak and the cross and candlesticks were specially designed in England, based on those at St Martins-in-the-Field Church in Trafalgar Square, London.

The Chapel, which can accommodate thirty people, is a popular location for weddings, with many couples enjoying the services of this special feature and also spending their honeymoon at the Hotel. For many years the Chapel was a focal point for the small local community, and traditional carols by candlelight are still sung in the Entrance Courtyard each Christmas.

The Hotel Chapel

Foundation for the Future

The redevelopment of the Hotel buildings created the foundations of the Hotel as we know it today. New laundry buildings were also built and additional water and power infrastructure installed to cope with the increased demands of the expanded Hotel. The buildings now covered a substantial area, presenting an additional challenge in managing room services for guests. In May 1931 Mr J R Hobson published a short account of the new hotel buildings in the Railway Company's staff bulletin

"A traveller revisiting the Victoria Falls after an absence of a few years will be surprised at the growth of the Hotel building and the general improvement in the service. No pains have been spared in effecting these improvements, and the results can best be appreciated by a personal visit.

"In the Victoria Falls Hotel main building there are various types of rooms; single rooms, single rooms with private bathroom attached, double rooms, double rooms with private bathrooms attached, and private suites comprising double bedroom, sitting room and bathroom, varying in price according to the accommodation offered, but all well furnished and well equipped.

"Every bedroom is fitted with an electric fan and with an electric bell system which operates an electric light outside the door. This light remains on until the

The Hotel Dining Room

call for service has been answered. The call is also automatically indicated in the office, and if a call remains unanswered for an appreciable time the fact can be observed from the office and rectified.

"The Restaurant is spacious and can accommodate a large number of casual visitors in addition to the full complement of residents in the hotel On occasions the Restaurant is used for dances; between 400 and 500 guests were present at the very successful cabaret held during the Easter holidays. The other public rooms comprise the Lounge, Summer Parlour Smoking Room, Drawing Room and Writing Room, each suitably furnished and equipped for its purpose. The Summer Parlour is situated upon the first floor and commands a very fine view of the Gorge and River. It provides an overflow space for the Lounge, but is not intended for dancing...

"From the verandah on the eastern side of the Lounge a beautiful panorama including the Gorge and the Bridge is obtained. While enjoying the grandeur and beauty of the Victoria Falls and appreciating the comfort of the Hotel, but few visitors will realised the continuous vigilance required to maintain the necessary service of pumping, lighting and refrigerating etc. The benefits of such services are only fully appreciated when for some reason they fail, though failures at the Victoria Falls Hotel are very rare occurrences." (Rhodesia Railways Bulletin, May 1931)

Road Routes

During the period 1925 to 1928, a dirt road was constructed between Bulawayo and Victoria Falls, providing access to the area for the growing number of regional tourists travelling by motor-car, and by 1931 a Motor Service Station had been developed close to the Hotel, offering running repairs and spare parts.

"Only a limited amount of growth occurred in the decade between 1920 and 1930. Further additions were made to the Police Camp in 1921 and to the existing Hotel buildings. Within the Railway Reserve, additional housing, government buildings and an African location were constructed west of the railway line and, towards the end of this period, a garage was built by the Railways in the north east portion of the Reserve." (Heath, 1977)

Mr Edward Herbert ('Ted') Spencer was initially posted to the Falls in April 1923 after joining the British South Africa Police. He soon saw the potential of a motor garage and car hire business, 'Spencer's Garage and Service Station,' to service the growing numbers of vehicles arriving at the Falls.

Flight of Angels

In the late 1920s a further transport innovation gave guests to the Victoria Falls Hotel a new and breath-taking way to experience the Falls, from the air - the 'Flight of Angels.' The short-lived Rhodesian Aviation Company was established with the aim of tapping the tourism potential of the Falls, with their first aircraft, an Avro Avian (VP-YAC), operating commercial 'flips' over the Victoria Falls from June 1929 (McAdams, 1969).

Henry Balfour, on his last of visits to the Falls in 1929 recorded:

"Great changes since 1910. A large and very fine stone hotel has replaced the wood and tin shanties which used to serve as [the] *hotel. I went down to the Aerodrome and... went up with Major Smith in an Avro-Avian plane. Flew over the Falls, down to beyond the Masui River and up as far as Kandahar Island. Wonderfully interesting. We flew at about 1,500 ft.* [457.2 m] *Made a very good take-off and landing."* (Balfour, 1929)

The Falls from above

Aeroplanes came to the rescue of stranded Hotel guests during a rail strike which took effect on 16th February 1929. The strike, combined with the rains which made the rough road from Bulawayo impassable, left the Falls completely isolated:

"Aeroplanes to the rescue. In this case it is to help a party of British tourists stranded at Victoria Falls owing to a strike in connection with the Rhodesian Railway. Even motor-cars were of no use, apparently, and the 'evacuation' arrangements had to rest upon aeroplanes." (Flight Magazine, 1929)

Those not evacuated by air extended their stay at the Hotel until the 2nd March when the first passenger train left the Falls for the south (Rhodesia Railways Bulletin, April 1929). The strike must have caused headaches for the Hotel's Head Chef, who relied on the train service to deliver the catering supplies from Bulawayo.

Aerial view of the Hotel with Court and West Wings complete

Spencer Airways

In July 1935 Ted Spencer purchased a second-hand De Havilland Puss Moth aircraft, ZS-ACB (re-registered as VP-YBC), and employed the services of a recently qualified young pilot Jack McAdam, to offer game viewing and charter flights from the Falls under the name of 'Spencer's Garage and Air Service' (later simply Spencer Airways). Flights operated from the Victoria Falls airfield, which would later become the Sprayview Aerodrome. In early 1936 Spencer acquired a DH.83 Fox Moth biplane (VP-YBD), in which he trained and soon qualified as a pilot. Spencer is recorded practising aerobatics and amazing his grounded African spectators - so much so that 'Spensaar' became an exclamation of amazement (Whitehead, 2014).

Spencer became something of a local legend in the Falls, and it is popularly believed that he was the first to fly a plane under the Victoria Falls Bridge, although McAdam is on record as discounting this story. There is, however, a photograph of him flying incredibly low over the Devil's Cataract. In his police patrol days Spencer is remembered casually riding his horse up the front steps of the Hotel, through the Lounge and Courtyard, up the steps to the Reception Hall and out of the Main Entrance (Kernan, 1984).

Puss Moth VP-YBC above the Falls

Bathing Costumes and Mackintoshes

With the 1930s defined by the Great Depression, the longest and most severe worldwide economic depression of the twentieth century, global tourism growth slowed significantly. Regional travel to the Falls was encouraged by the Railway Company with the offer of inclusive travel and accommodation fares, with passengers staying at the Hotel. Special fares were not available for the busy public holiday periods when the Hotel was still well patronised and often ran a long waiting list. A 1930s Southern Rhodesian government guide to the Victoria Falls contained the following advice for visitors to the Falls:

> *"Visitors are advised to provide themselves with mackintoshes and galoshes (boots) when traversing the Rain Forest, or when exposed to the spray-clouds. Oilskins and sou'-westers can be hired from the Hotel... When spray from the Falls is heavy, visitors will find it an advantage to wear a bathing costume only underneath the mackintosh."* (Martin, 1997)

Clothing advice for tourists recommended sunshades for the ladies and wide-brimmed felt hats for gentlemen. Swimming, golf (Livingstone Golf Course opened in 1909), tennis, and fishing were all listed as available leisure and sports activities, and a 15 minute flight over the Falls cost £1. The pioneering travel agent Thomas Cook promoted the Falls in 1930 as a fashionable destination:

> *"There is a splendid and comfortable Hotel at the Falls and during the season the fashionable throngs in the grounds and on the verandas are*

Bathers at the Falls

more reminiscent of a European spa than of a retreat in the interior of Africa." (McGregor, 2009)

In place of rowdy payday railway and Bridge engineers, elegant black-tie Saturday night dinner dances were now the regular routine.

"Two bands were used in the Dining Room - one at either end so that as one finished a tune, the other would start another... The furniture was all natural cane - very cool and very gracious. Beds were 4-posters and mosquito nets hung right over the top and straight down the sides. If one took the trolley ride to the Falls, on the return journey the men would get off and help push the trolley back up the hill - ladies would remain seated." (Henderson, undated)

In 1936 Mr Ward retired as Manager of the Hotel, after 28 years service with the Railway Company and almost 14 years at the Hotel, being replaced by Mr Thomas Grant Colquhoun.

An update in the Rhodesia Railways Bulletin, November 1938, describes the Hotel:

"The Hotel is now able to accommodate 160 persons, there being six private suites and 105 bedrooms, about half of which have private bathrooms. All rooms have been equipped with electric fans and all doors and windows are covered with mosquito gauze. The bedroom furniture throughout the Hotel has been specially imported from overseas, the majority of it being of oak.

The Hotel staff, December 1930

In two sections of the Hotel, however, the bedroom furniture is of walnut and Spanish mahogany respectively. It is generally conceded that the Victoria Falls Hotel ranks amongst the leading hotels in the continent of Africa. The nature of the accommodation it offers, the quality of its catering and the efficiency of its service are all the more remarkable in a place so far removed from those centres where the modern refinements of the hotelier's craft are available.

"There are 19 Europeans, 3 Indians and 196 natives employed at the Hotel. To secure efficiency of service, the staff is so arranged that Europeans are in immediate control of various sections. The head waiter, who supervises the dining room, capable of seating 250 people, has the help of an assistant controlling the work of 27 waiters and 13 pantrymen. The kitchen staff comprises three chefs, and apprentice cook and 18 natives. There are two housekeepers who have control of 37 bedroom boys and 5 hall boys. The head porter has charge of 18 natives in the baggage services, the collection of stores and provisions and the tidying of the Hotel grounds. The European in charge of the linen room is responsible for the laundry, which is staffed by an Indian laundryman and 15 natives. An Indian gardener is employed for the upkeep of the Hotel lawns, a citrus orchard and the cultivation of flowers; he has a gang of 15 natives for this work. The trolley cars that work between the Hotel and the Falls are operated by 17 natives, who come under the supervision of the European boatman, as do also the 13 natives employed on the boating services. There is a night porter, who has four native watchmen to assist him, as well as a waiter for the serving of any light refreshments required after midnight.

"Apart from the manager, the Hotel office staff numbers four and there are two barmen and a storekeeper. In addition to all these employees engaged in the actual running of the various Hotel services, there is an electrician always available to supervise the lighting of the Hotel and the working of the ice plant.

"Although the Hotel is 280 miles [450 km] away from the nearest market of any consequence, catering arrangements have been so organised that they have become comparatively simple. From the number of advance booking received an estimate is made of the number of visitors expected at the Hotel a week ahead and requisitions for supplies are complied accordingly, requirements being met from the Catering Department Store at Bulawayo. All perishable commodities are sent to the Hotel three times weekly, with the exception of milk, which is sent daily. Particular care is taken to see that all supplies travel under the best possible conditions, milk for example being despatched in specially made thermos cans. General stores are supplied once a month.

"The Hotel comes under the Acting Catering Superintendent of the Rhodesia Railways, Mr P Shinn, and the staff, under the manager, Mr T G Colquhoun, are particularly conscious of its good reputation. They are zealous, therefore, each in his or her own particular sphere, to ensure that every visitor leaves the Hotel with a sense of satisfaction." (Rhodesia Railways Bulletin, November 1938)

All in a Day's Work

According to an unattributed and undated account, the Hotel management sought the advice of Ted Davison, the senior game warden at Wankie (now Hwange) National Park, for help with the ongoing problem of the resident baboons. 'Problem' animals can loose their fear of humans and become dangerous, and the last resort is to cull key individuals in the hope that the rest of the troop change their habits and avoid the Hotel grounds. Highly intelligent, they soon become wary of those intending them harm, and Davison attempted various methods to get close to his quarry before sitting at one of the tables on the lawn with a newspaper in front of him, through which he had cut a hole to watch his prey:

"When a suitable specimen got close enough he drew his revolver, but somehow the trigger got caught and he shot himself in the leg. Not wanting to draw attention to his carelessness he got up and walked to the hotel, only realising afterward that he had left a trail of blood across the veranda and lounge."

Twin Room

The account goes on to highlight some of the more unusual challenges for the Hotel management.

"In the early hours of a Sunday morning the Hotel Manager was woken by sounds of hilarity coming from the pool. On investigating he discovered a party of young Livingstonians having a nude bathing party. He quietly collected all their clothes and took these to his office. There were many tales of how these young folk managed to get home to Livingstone. A notice was inserted in the Livingstone Mail to the effect that those people who had left their clothes behind could collect them by calling personally at the Manager's Office. As far as I know none were ever collected."

Another incident involved a party of Oxford and Cambridge graduates who dined at the Hotel one evening:

"After a very good meal they gathered in the lounge in high spirits. Somehow a rugby match started with a cushion being used as a ball. This didn't impress the Manager, but when he tried to intervene he suddenly found himself being rolled up in the carpet! Fortunately one of the more sober men unrolled the carpet before he suffocated. After apologies all parted in good spirits." (Anon, undated)

The Hotel Veranda

The Smoking Room

Devil of the Cataract

In January 1934 newspapers around the world printed a story under the sensational headline 'Monster In Zambesi - Lives in Cataract At Foot of Victoria Falls.' At least four Europeans living at the Falls claimed to have witnessed the serpent of the Falls, including Victor Pare who had now seen the mysterious creature for a second time, and its existence appears to have been prematurely 'confirmed' by Captain J J Reynard, the curator of the Falls.

> *"A monster 30ft [9.1m] long with a small head and a thick black body is the description given by the natives of the devil of Devils Cataract, Victoria Falls, on the Zambesi River, Rhodesia, which has been seen twice by Mr Victor Pare at the foot of the cataract. It has also been seen by others at Danger Point. The monster is mentioned by the late Dr Livingstone (who discovered the Falls in 1855) and its existence is confirmed by the Government curator who thinks it probable that there are several of them."* (Melbourne Argus, January 1934)

Indeed, Livingstone recorded local belief in a mythical river serpent which could hold a canoe in its grasp or capsize its paddlers.

> *"The Barotse believe that at certain parts of the river a tremendous monster lies*

hid, and that it will catch a canoe, and hold it fast and motionless, in spite of the utmost exertions of the paddlers." (Livingstone, 1857)

Some early residents of Livingstone even claimed to have seen the great serpent writhing in the torrents of the river below the Falls.

"In 1905 a large black serpent-like creature was seen by several residents and this was linked to the traditional monster which Africans have always feared as lurking in the depths of the gorge." (Harris, 1969)

Six months later Captain Reynard was still convinced of his story.

"Meet 'the devil' of Devil's Cataract, Southern Rhodesia, the latest rival to that elusive monster of Loch Ness. He is described by Captain J J Reynard, curator of the Southern Rhodesian section of the Victoria Falls, where the Devil's Cataract is situated, as a beast 30 feet [9.1m] long, with a small head and a thick, black body. At least four Europeans living at the Falls have seen this monster, Captain Reynard declared while on holiday in Durban, and Mr Victor Pare, who has lived on the banks of the Zambesi for 13 years has seen it twice. Mr Pare has described how he saw 'fold after fold' of the monster before it disappeared mysteriously beneath the water. 'In the minds of the natives,' added Captain Reynard, 'there is no doubt of the reality of the monster, and it has apparently been a tribal bogey for many generations.'" (Kalgoorlie Miner, June 1934)

In 1938 a guidebook to the Falls recorded more cautiously:

"The Zambezi can boast of no Loch Ness monster, although there is an old tradition among the Barotse that a serpent, called by them 'Lingangole,' had its habitation in the Zambezi river, which it left at night only. There are stories even today of a huge serpent, thirty feet [9.1m] in length, which is said to be visible occasionally at the bottom of the gorge." (Southern Rhodesia Publicity Office, 1938)

Visit of Prince George

His Royal Highness Prince George (soon after to become the Duke of Kent), the fourth son of King George V, visited the Falls in 1934 as part of a tour of southern Africa. The Prince travelled to the Cape by the Union Castle Carnervon Castle, the South African Railways again providing the use of the special 'White Train' for the tour. Staying at the Hotel, the Prince spent the Easter weekend exploring the Falls:

The Prince's Bedroom

"A mile [1.6 km] wide and with a drop of four hundred feet [120 m], the Falls presented an inspiring sight when the Prince, changing into a vest and shorts soon after his arrival, hurried from the Hotel to have a first look at them. The Zambesi was coming down in flood, and enormous quantities of water were hurtling over the Falls... During the weekend the river steadily rose as the result of rain in the heart of Africa, and when the Prince left the Falls two days later, it had reached a new record high level. Because of the vast volume of water pouring into the chasm the spray was very dense, and somewhat obscured the view but the Prince spent so much time around the Falls that he saw every possible aspect of them. Declining to use a waterproof coat, His Royal Highness thoroughly explored the wonders of the Rain Forest, in which he wandered about opposite the Main Cataract until he was drenched to the skin.

"The Prince spent many hours energetically visiting every vantage point, despite the uncomfortable heat. He was particularly impressed by the lunar rainbow... The Prince did a lot of walking in the countryside around the Hotel, the whole area being a game reserve and abounding with animals and birds. But the Prince unfortunately did not see any crocodiles, which thrive on the Zambesi River. The flood waters had driven the reptiles way." (Frew, 1934)

It was recorded in the Rhodesia Railways Bulletin that Chief Steward J B Higgins and Steward C Redmond waited upon the Prince during his stay at the Hotel

(Rhodesia Railways Bulletin, March 1934). Prince George served as an R.A.F. officer from the late 1930s. He died in a military air-crash on 25th August 1942, on board a R.A.F. Short Sunderland flying boat in Scotland, at the age of 39.

Inclusive Excursions

Special inclusive fare excursions to Victoria Falls with accommodation at the Falls Hotel, advertised for both first and second class travel, were always popular. Initially restricted to departures from Bulawayo and Salisbury (now Harare), in the mid-1930s these were extended to other regional centres in the country. Such special fare trips were not available at Easter, July and Christmas holiday seasons, when the Hotel was always fully booked and had a long waiting list for cancellations (Croxton, 1982). In July 1934 the Rhodesia Railways Bulletin published the following anonymous letter forwarded from the Falls Hotel.

"I feel I must write and congratulate your Railways' wonderful effort in the combined excursion at £5 10s. 0d. for the Rhodes and Founders holidays. It is beyond comprehension and that of several other people I have spoken to, how it is done for the money. With such crowds of people one would expect inefficiency and bad service, but nowhere have we had but the very best of attention and everything we wanted. The catering in the trains and Hotel was really excellent and calls for great credit for the organisation. In conclusion I feel I have to thank you for this lovely holiday for which I don't think I have paid half enough. It certainly is the best value I have struck for years."

The article concluded:

"This unqualified testimony of the value which the Railways offer should encourage all employees to recommend to the public, whenever suitable opportunities occur, the inclusive excursions to the Victoria Falls." (Rhodesia Railways Bulletin, July 1934)

Wings of War

During the Second World War (1939-45) the Falls Hotel played host to many Allied soldiers and airmen receiving their basic training in the country. Bulawayo was a major centre for the Royal Air Force Training Group with several Flying Training Schools for trainee airmen from across the British Commonwealth. An estimated 8,500 British Royal Air Force (R.A.F.) crew were trained in Southern Rhodesia over the period of the war, and training continued into the post-war period.

The Falls was one of several official recreational leave locations, and the Hotel offered special half-rates to R.A.F. recruits. One such guest airman was Australian pilot Mr Colin Johnston who stayed at the Hotel in the early 1940s. In 2013 his son returned a Hotel room key which had been found amongst his possessions after his death - seventy years after his stay (Zambezi Traveller, December 2013). Another young recruit to the R.A.F. Training School in Bulawayo

1940s Hotel key

was Christopher Lee (later Sir), who would later find fame as a stage and film actor - a career which would bring him back to the Falls Hotel some 45 years later.

The Hotel was regularly fully booked over public holiday weekends, to the extent that trains standing in the railway sidings still accommodated the occasional overflow of guests.

> *"In the period between the two World Wars the patronage never quite reached the 8,000 mark, but with the large numbers of visitors from the Forces during World War II the numbers climbed, reaching 9,700 by 1945 and jumping to more than 11,000 two years later."* (Rhodesia Railways Magazine, October 1967)

Spencer Tragedies

Towards the end of the war Spencer's Airways were operating a fleet of four different aircraft, including a Tiger Moth to provide short pleasure trips over the Falls, and a larger Fairchild UC.61A for longer-distance game viewing flights. Ted Spencer died in a tragic accident at Croydon Airport, London, in early 1947 when the Dakota plane he was piloting crashed on take-off.

Ted's nephew, Terrance, took over the family business. Having survived flying a Lancaster bomber through the war, he died almost two years after his uncle, in October 1948, in another tragic crash. Whilst on a game flight with three tourist passengers, the Fairchild caught fire somewhere over the Katambora Rapids, crashing into woodland on the remote Westwood Farm. The crash site took six weeks to locate (Meadows, 2000).

Mr Tones Calls the Tune

Mr Vincent Tones took over the management reins at the Hotel in the mid-1940s, transferred to the post from the Railways Catering Department, and remaining as manager until 1961.

> *"Mild manners, poker-faced, extremely courteous to guests and staff, his demeanour and outward appearance hides one of the most efficient hotel personalities in the Federation. He is the hotelkeeper's ideal hotelier. Nothing seems to disturb his calm. His staff respect and admire him. At mealtimes he himself walks round the dining-room asking guests whether there is anything lacking in the service of the Hotel."* (Aberman, 1955)

Mr Tones was the first Rhodesian-born manager of the Hotel and was to oversee an immediate transformation of the Hotel's fortunes. For most of its life to date the Hotel had often failed to break-even, let alone post of profit.

During the 1948-49 financial year the Hotel made a record operating profit of

Mr Tones

£15,205 (substantially greater than the previous record profit of £8,069 recorded in 1929), and a total income of £120,688, again a significant increase on the record of the previous year. Visitor arrivals, also a record, totalled 21,014, representing 49,707 bed-nights.

Presenting his annual report to the Victoria Falls Hotel Company Board, Sir Arthur Griffin, Chairman, moved *"that the Railways be requested to convey the appreciation of the meeting to the Manager of the Hotel and to his staff for their excellent services during the past year in maintaining the high standard of the Hotel"* (Victoria Falls Hotel Ltd, 1950).

Analysis of the Hotel's 16,998 visitors hosted during 1948 showed that 6,906 came from South Africa, 4,071 from the United Kingdom, 3,965 Southern Rhodesia, 637 Northern Rhodesia, and 252 from the United States. Other nations recorded included Brazil, China and Russia (Rhodesia Railways Bulletin, March 1949).

The Royal Family Visit the Falls

In 1947 the British Royal Tour of the Union of South Africa and the Rhodesias included a visit to the Victoria Falls, with Their Majesties King George VI, Queen Elizabeth and their two daughters, Their Royal Highnesses the Princess Elizabeth (now the reigning monarch, Her Majesty Queen Elizabeth II) and Princess Margaret, staying at the Hotel, which was commandeered entirely for their use.

The tour was arranged as a 'thank you' to General Smuts and the people of South Africa for their support during the Second World War (more than 11,000 South African's lost their lives during the War), being the first overseas state visit since 1939. Princess Elizabeth celebrated her 21st birthday during the tour. South African Railways provided a newly built 'White Train,' the Garratt locomotives of which were painted deep royal blue and which were used throughout the tour of Rhodesia.

A great deal of planning was undertaken to ensure that the Hotel would be worthy of the very high honour of providing a temporary home for the Royal Family.

"At the Victoria Falls the whole of the station platform was given a tar macadam surface, as well as the extensive car parking area and various paths around the Hotel, including the approach road to the Hotel front door... Special work was also done by the [Railway] *Mechanical Department to place the two launches 'Daphne' and 'Diana' in the best possible condition for the journey of the Royal Family across the Zambesi River from the Southern Rhodesia side to Northern Rhodesia."* (Rhodesia Railways Bulletin, April 1947)

The Royal Party view the Falls

Preparations for the visit involved extensive upgrading works to the Hotel buildings and refurbishment of rooms.

Items of expenditure included 257 Lloyd Loom wicker chairs, with 53 matching tables and 28 linen baskets, 30 chairs and ten tables for the Dining Room, and 18 new beds with mattresses, and the painting of a flower themed mural in the Dining Room. Improvements to the grounds included resurfacing of the approach road and parking areas, and erection of garages for the small fleet of support vehicles (Victoria Falls Hotel Ltd, 1948).

> *"They arrived at the Victoria Falls Hotel, which was to be their home for the next few days, just before noon on Friday, April 11th, and after greeting Sir John and Lady Kennedy* [the Governor of Southern Rhodesia and his wife]*, who had come on ahead to receive them, went out at once to get their first view of the grandest natural spectacle in Africa."*

The visit was a welcome break following many public engagements during the tour, and repeated visits were made to the Falls.

> *"The Royal Family visited the Falls on two separate days. They saw them under the sun and under the moon, from the level of the upper river, and from that of the gorge. They walked through the so-called 'Rain Forest' opposite the Main Falls, where the spray forms a perpetual cloud, and where the King remarked that for the first time in his life he had been soaked even through his hat."*
> (Morrah, 1947)

Their Majesties' suite was on the first floor of the south wing, which for many years after was known as the Queen's Suite, and the suite of Princess Elizabeth and Princess Margaret was located on the ground floor of the same wing.

The Royal Party on the Hotel's launch, the 'Daphne'

"The weather... even in April, was 'boiling,' preventing the King from relaxing, although in a rare private photograph both Princesses can be seen in bathing suits lying around the pool with the younger members of the Household."
(Viney, 2018)

On 12th April 1947, the day dubbed by the Livingstone Mail as the *"most important day in the history of the town,"* the Royal Party visited Livingstone, for the afternoon at least, crossing the river in the Hotel's launch, 'Daphne.' Flying the Royal Standard, the party sailed up to the Zambezi Boat Club on the northern bank, escorted upstream by the state barge of Barotseland Paramount Chief, Litunga Imwiko. The road from the river was re-named the Royal Mile in honour of the occasion.

"From the point of view of watchers on the northern bank, where Sir John Waddington, the Governor of Northern Rhodesia, was waiting, the launch flying the royal banner came into view round the eastern end of the largest of the many islands, called Long Island, and simultaneously, from the mouth of the tributary Maramba, appeared the state barge of Imwiko, Paramount Chief of the Barotse, the largest group of tribes in Northern Rhodesia." (Morrah, 1947)

Staying at the Hotel over the Easter weekend, the Royal party celebrated divine service at the Hotel chapel on Sunday 13th April. Sir Arthur Griffin, Chairman of the Victoria Falls Hotel Company Board, reported at their 34th Ordinary General Meeting, held in February the following year:

"These few days afforded the Royal Family the opportunity of a complete rest after their strenuous tour through South Africa and Southern Rhodesia, and appreciation was expressed by His Majesty of the excellent arrangements made for their welfare and comfort." (Victoria Falls Hotel Ltd, 1948)

Later in the tour, in a famous speech broadcast from Cape Town on her twenty-first birthday, 21st April 1947, the young Princess Elizabeth dedicated her life to the service of the Commonwealth. It was only recently discovered that the speech was pre-recorded by the Princess during her stay at the Hotel, and not broadcast from Cape Town as had previously been thought. In a diary kept by the King's press secretary, Captain Lewis Ritchie, it is recorded that on Sunday 13th April 1947 whilst staying at the Victoria Falls:

"At 6 p.m, Princess Elizabeth recorded her speech for the B.B.C. It was afterwards played off for Her Royal Highness to hear and was a great triumph." (Hardman, 2018)

A reminder of the Royal visit remains in a far corner of the grounds beyond the tennis courts, where a large plinth stands alone, bearing a plaque:

"This platform was used by H.R.H. King George VI and H.R.H. Queen Elizabeth and Their Royal Highnesses, Princess Elizabeth and Princes Margaret, during a garden party held in April 1947. The Royal Party were guests at the Victoria Falls Hotel."

Several islands and special locations were renamed after the Royal visit:

"His late Majesty, King George VI expressed a desire to have some of the islands in the Zambesi named after his family; Long Island [also known as Siloka or Loando Island] *was renamed King George VI Island, Kalai Island became Queen Elizabeth Island, Siachikola Island became Princess Elizabeth Island... His Majesty also renamed Dale's Kopje, Queen Elizabeth Kopje."*
(Clark, 1952)

The tradition was started in 1904 with the renaming of three large islands; 'Princess Christian' and 'Princess Victoria' after the visits of Princess Christian and Victoria, and 'Kandahar' after the visit of Lord Roberts. The Hotel's landing stage was also named in honour of the visit, becoming known as the King's Landing Stage and Boat House. In 1955 Her Royal Highness Princess Marie Louise visited Livingstone and the Falls, also having an island renamed after her.

The Flying Boat Service

In 1946 the British Overseas Airways Corporation (B.O.A.C.), successor to Imperial Airways, introduced the famous Short S.45 Solent class of flying boat, and in May 1948 a new trans-Africa airmail and passenger route was launched from Southampton to Vaaldam, Johannesburg. Initially operating twice-weekly (later increased to three services), the new 'Springbok Service' replaced the Short S.23 'C Class' Empire flying boats which had operated the east coast route to Durban from 1937, covering the new route in four days. There was no flying at night, and the route included overnight stops in Sicily, Luxor, Kampala and Victoria Falls.

The low-flying Solents weighed 35 tons and were powered by four Bristol Hercules engines with a cruising speed of 210 mph. The aircraft carried a crew of seven and up to 34 passengers plus mail and cargo. Tickets for the 6,350 mile (10,219 km) journey were advertised at £167 single and £300 12s return.

The flying boats landed, and were serviced, on a wide flat stretch of the Zambezi River some seven kilometres upstream of the Falls, stretching 2,500 yards (2,286 metres) in length, and 500 yards (457 metres) wide. Construction of a terminal reception, landing stage and jetty, as well as a road linking with the Victoria Falls

Solent flying boat on the Zambezi

town and Hotel, had been completed in late 1947. The first Solent (G-AHIN 'Southampton') landed on the Zambezi on a test flight on 11th December 1947, and the first commercial service (G-AHIT 'Severn') departed Southampton on 4th May 1948, landing on the Zambezi on the 8th. Raymond Critchell was one of the six-man fire and emergency rescue team based on the south bank of the Zambezi:

"The B.O.A.C. Base comprised of a small group of buildings with the usual offices, workshops and passenger facilities on the southern River bank, with an unmade road some four miles [6.4 km] long connecting this to the Vic Falls 'village.' There was also a locally made bus 'garage' for a pair of passenger coaches owned by B.O.A.C. This was a thatched roof spanning between several palm trees, just to keep the coaches cool, and which the local elephants took pleasure in knocking down periodically. There was a pier leading down to the river, with a hinged gangway from the pier down to a floating landing stage, which allowed for the rise and fall of the river, and from which passengers embarked into launches." (Critchell, 2007)

The stopover at the Victoria Falls Hotel soon became one of the highlights of the route for those few lucky enough to experience the journey, and the stretch of river and terminal reception where the planes landed became affectionately known as the 'Jungle Junction,' a nickname apparently first given by a reporter from the Bulawayo Chronicle.

"These wonderful aircraft... represented the best and most luxurious form of transport at that time. They were two decked, with comfortable seating, quite unlike today's aircraft, even providing a couple of four-seater cabins on the lower deck. There was a powder room for the ladies with a make up table,

complete with illuminated mirror, and the top range of make up and accessories were provided free of charge. There was a cocktail lounge, complete with a well stocked bar where you could sit on a high bar stool and watch the ground slowly unroll below through large windows, whilst sipping the drink of your choice." (Critchell, 2007)

The Hotel was responsible for providing the onboard catering for the return journey. Food rationing was still in force in England after the war and the passengers were apparently always impressed by the sumptuous catering on board.

In the early 1950s the Victoria Falls community was still not much more than a village, Critchell continuing:

"Around this time... I met a chap, ...[Syd] Brown, who operated the Hotel tourist launch, which carries guests up the river. This was a very posh affair, all polished brass and varnish, with a shady canopy to keep the sun off. He had also been a signalman and used to call us up on his signal lamp to ask when the aircraft was due in so that he could pull well into the river bank. He would also pass on details of any dolly birds he had on board in case anyone from B.O.A.C. wanted to go down the pub that night to meet them. The community was centred around the hotel which had quite a large staff, the Railway Station with an on-site Post Office, the Vic Falls Conservator who lived at the small government camping site, a Police/Customs/Immigration post, and of course, the ubiquitous Trading Store." (Critchell, 2007)

The period of the flying boats was, however, brief, operating for just over two and a half years before being overtaken by the development of a new generation of pressurised aircraft. The Solent service ended in November 1950, replaced with the Hermes airliner which completed the journey between London and Johannesburg (via the new Livingstone airport) in just under a day and a half.

The site of the Jungle Junction was commemorated by British Airways in December 1982 with the erection of a cairn, and is remembered in the name of the Hotel's current outdoor buffet restaurant. A mural at the Main Entrance also celebrates this unique period of aviation transport:

"This mural commemorates the weekly flying boat service between Southampton and Johannesburg set up in 1948. The Solents... landed and were serviced on a reach of the Zambezi above the Victoria Falls, permitting an overnight at this Hotel, the stop being affectionately know to all as the Jungle Junction."

The Hotel swimming pool

All Black Mischief

Critchell also recalls a passing incident involving the visit of the New Zealand rugby team during their tour of South Africa in 1949:

> *"Amongst the other few permanent residents* [of Victoria Falls] *were Mr and Mrs Clark, owners of Clark's Curio Stores... They had a pool with small live crocodiles in it, and a couple of quite large stuffed ones hanging on the wall. On one occasion, which coincided with a visit from the All Blacks rugby touring team, one of the stuffed ones found itself in the Vic Falls Hotel swimming pool."* (Critchell, 2007)

By this time Percy Clark's son, Victor, had taken over his late father's business. Rhodesia won a celebrated victory in Bulawayo, and drew the match in Salisbury, although many key New Zealand players were not part of the tour due to apartheid restrictions in South Africa.

Into the Fifties

On 1st April 1947 the Rhodesian Government acquired the assets of the Rhodesia Railways Limited, the Railway Company subsequently becoming a statutory body known as Rhodesia Railways on 1st November 1949. The Railway management now answered to the higher authority of central government under the Ministry of Transport.

In late 1949 it was reported that the hotel was making an estimated loss of £1,000 every month, despite the rising numbers of tourists and increasing American market (The Sydney Sun, December 1949).

Despite the operational losses, attention soon focussed on expanding the Hotel:

"For several years the capacity of the Victoria Falls Hotel has been inadequate to meet the increasing demands for accommodation. The hotel contains 104 bedrooms comprising 53 singles (12 with bathrooms), 46 doubles (21 with bathrooms) and five suites capable of accommodating 155 visitors. By providing additional beds in certain of the rooms, however, it has been possible to accommodate 185 people during holiday periods...

"In consequence large numbers of prospective visitors have been turned away, not only during the 'season,' which was formerly reckoned as the months of May to September, but also during the remaining months of the year, which were generally considered to be in the 'off season.'

"It has been evident for some time that the hotel should be extended but, owing to the war and to the subsequent restrictions placed on buildings of this nature, it has only recently been possible to secure the necessary permit. After considering several schemes, it was finally decided to construct a second storey on the West Wing and the Court, or North connecting wing,

The Hotel Courtyard

which are situated on that portion of the hotel nearest to the entrance from the Victoria Falls station. When completed the extensions will make available 24 additional bedrooms, and will accommodate a further 54 visitors, or a total of 128 bedrooms with accommodation for 209 people or, by 'doubling-up' during the holiday periods, a total of 245 visitors. All the bedrooms on the ground floor affected by the extensions will be provided with a bathroom, as also will the additional bedrooms to be constructed on the second storey. Provision has also been made for a Conference Room over the present Entrance Halls, which will be approached by two staircases, for the use of which there is an increasing demand by municipalities and various societies." (Rhodesia Railways Bulletin, February 1950)

The works were undertaken by local contractor Carlo Gardini, beginning a long working association with the Hotel. Two spiral staircases were also constructed running up to the second floor Summer Parlour, an impressive work of craftsmanship, if yet slightly out of character with the Hotel's original architectural style. The conference room was named the Pullman Suite after the well known Pullman rail cars. The room would become an important venue for influential meetings and conferences and also doubled as a cinema:

"The weekly dances and bi-weekly cinema shows continue to be exceptionally popular and are all well attended. The cinema shows, which include films of natural interest, are held in the new conference room and the dances in the main lounge." (Rhodesia Railways Magazine, May 1952)

Dance floor crowds

The Hotel's Laundry was also the focus of renovations and modernisation to cope with increasing numbers of guests:

"An essential requirement for any modern hotel is a well equipped laundry. The existing laundry was erected many years ago, and is inadequate for present needs. A new and large laundry is to be provided with up-to-date sorting, ironing and washing facilities, together with suitable changing rooms and accessible sanitary arrangements for the African staff. Orders have been place overseas for the most modern washing, drying, ironing and pressing machines, and the new laundry should then be capable of dealing efficiently and hygienically with the large volume of work to be done for the hotel and for its visitors.

"Work on the extensions to the Court, or North connecting wing, and on the new laundry is now in hand, and it is hoped the former will be completed by April. The remainder of the extensions will be carried out so as to cause as little inconvenience to visitors as possible. The total estimated cost of the extensions, including equipment, is over £100,000." (Rhodesia Railways Bulletin, February 1950)

Attention now turned to the main public areas of the Hotel, including the Lounge areas and Dining Room, and plans included extensions to both rooms. In an article detailing the work of the Railway's catering department it was recorded that for the operational year ending March 1950 the Hotel recorded 21,052 guests, its highest ever total, and served 52,567 breakfasts, 51,170 luncheons, and 56,528 dinners. In addition 11,222 lunches were provided to passengers carried to Kandahar Island on the Hotel's launches (Rhodesia Railways Bulletin, February 1951).

"By 1950 the hotel was enjoying boom conditions, the completion of building extensions, the introduction of the B.O.A.C. flying-boat service and patronage by American passengers from several luxury world cruise ships, rocketing the figure up to 21,052 [visitors]." (Rhodesia Railways Magazine, October 1967)

As a result of the Southern Rhodesia Companies Act 1951, in July 1952 the Victoria Falls Hotel Ltd, by Special Resolution, adopted updated Articles of Association, becoming The Victoria Falls Hotel (Private) Limited. In the same year, after some investigation into the matter, the General Manager of the Railway Company reported that no justification or benefit would arise by passing the control of the Hotel to local management, as opposed to the Catering Department of the Railways. The Catering Department enabled economic central purchasing of supplies and administration of accounts and personnel, although constrained by Railway employment regulations.

Relaxing in the Lounge

A Wasted Opportunity

Despite expenditure being approved for a more efficient sewage system, the Falls Hotel decided upon the installation a of smaller and cheaper sewage facility which, after very basic filtering, discharged processed sewage down a pipeline running through the forth gorge and directly into the Zambezi.

"Shareholders have previously been advised that the Board originally approved an estimated expenditure of £5,000 for the provision of a modern sewage disposal plant, and that an alternative scheme was being investigated of running the sewage from the Hotel into a specially designed septic tank and the effluent there from direct into the Zambezi River in the Forth Gorge. This alternative scheme has now been approved by the Government authorities and work will be commenced shortly. The cost is only £1,400 after making allowance for the demolition of the existing assets, and I am assured that the scheme will be just as satisfactory as the more expensive modern plant originally proposed." (Victoria Falls Hotel Ltd, 1950)

Quiet Luxury

"When you come up each day from the Falls, awed by the thunder of the world's greatest river wonder - thrilled by the splendour of the sunrise, the Lunar

Rainbow or, perhaps, the sight of hippo and crocodile... pleasantly tired... then it is that you fully appreciate the quiet luxury of the Victoria Falls Hotel, its efficient service and its excellent cuisine." (Victoria Falls Hotel, 1950s)

Schoolboy Shenanigans

The Bulawayo Chronicle for 22nd May 1950 published an article which detailed some of the escapades in which local schoolchildren indulged. At the commencement and end of each school term, the railways conveyed thousands of high-spirited boys and girls to and from their schools.

"An air of worried anticipation is noticeable at the Victoria Falls Hotel today (Sunday). Children on their way to Southern Rhodesia to school after an inter-term holiday pass through by train tonight. On previous occasions groups of up to 20 strong have shaken the Hotel's stately composure by quitting the train at Livingstone, commandeering taxis and driving at great speed the eight miles [12.9 km] to the hotel. They rejoin their train an hour or so later when it reaches the Falls station.

"School children's energy, their capacity to order and consume vast quantities of tea, cakes and sandwiches, their unconventional attire of sports shirts, shorts and slippers, and the noise they make are received by the Hotel staff with tolerant though apprehensive amusement." (Rhodesia Railways Bulletin, June 1950)

Breakfast in the Dining Room

Livingstone Joins the Jet-set

In 1950 Livingstone Airport was developed on a new site approximately three miles (4.8 km) to the north-west of the town, with a fully modernised control tower and tarmac runway. The opening ceremony for the new airport was performed by Lord Pakenham, Northern Rhodesia Minister of Civil Aviation, on 12th August 1950. It was proudly reported that the spray from the Victoria Falls could be seen from the control tower. The airport served as the main international gateway for the region, including guests of the Falls Hotel, until the opening of Salisbury Airport in 1956 and the subsequent development of the Victoria Falls Airport in 1967.

First Commercial Jet Passenger Flight

On 2nd May 1952 the 'Yoke Peter,' a de Havilland Comet Mark 1, took off from London Heathrow to Johannesburg on the world's first commercial passenger jet flight, proudly operated by B.O.A.C. The flight stopped for refuelling at Rome, Beirut, Khartoum, Entebbe and Livingstone before arriving in Johannesburg, a distance of 6,700 miles (10,782 km) in 18 hours 40 minutes flying time (and total journey time of 23 hours 20 minutes).

> *"The past few weeks have been full of interest for visitors to the Falls since the inauguration of the Comet Jet air service has brought a number of the 'bird men' to the hotel. Sir Milnes Thomas, B.O.A.C. Chief, flew in and out in April and, on an earlier plane, was 'Cat's Eyes' Cunningham of test pilot fame. Sir John de Albiac, Commandant of London Airport, also visited the Falls with several members of his staff."* (Rhodesia Railways Magazine, June 1952)

Growth of Commercial Airlines

The growth of long-haul commercial air travel opened up direct, and faster, travel to the Falls, further boosting tourism. International carriers serving Livingstone soon included B.O.A.C, Air France and South Africa Airways. For a period all passengers disembarked at Livingstone Airport to stay overnight at the Falls Hotel before either continuing their flight to South Africa or travelling by land to many of the National Parks and other destinations within the region.

The development of regional aviation routes, including those of Central African Airways (formed in 1946) during the 1950s, marked a significant development in tourist travel, breaking nearly fifty years of railway dominance. Despite this, the railway-owned and managed Falls Hotel continued to flourish during this period.

"One of the most remarkably successful innovations has been a Sunday excursion trip from Salisbury to Victoria Falls and back, 680 miles [1,094 km] for a return fare of £10, which includes a box lunch, a boat trip up the Zambesi to see elephant, hippo and crocodile, a coach trip to the Falls, and tea at the Victoria Falls Hotel before returning to Salisbury." (Flight Magazine, 1951)

Famous visitors to the Hotel during the fifties included many stars of the screen, including Grace Kelly, Anne Todd, Danny Kaye, and actor and comedian George Formby (who stayed at the Hotel during a 17-show tour of Southern Rhodesia in 1953). Actors Dana Andrews and Jeanne Crain stayed at the Hotel in 1953 during filming of the 'Duel in the Jungle,' and film-maker Alfred Hitchcock visited the Falls in 1956. The Hotel also offered screenings of the latest films in a room specially converted into a small cinema.

In order to integrate the arrival of passengers on commercial flights a new railway time-table was released and new routine established at the Falls Hotel.

"The new train time tables now in operation have completely reversed the routine at the hotel. Instead of the majority of passengers arriving at night they now get in before breakfast. All visitors from the south and from overseas are now making their reservations in good time rather than risk being disappointed." (Rhodesia Railways Magazine, July 1952)

Formation of Federation

Preliminary conferences on the proposed unification of Southern and Northern Rhodesia together with Nyasaland (now independent Malawi) were held at the Hotel in 1947, 1949 and 1951, followed by a series of conferences held in London during 1952/3. The three African governments, with negotiators from the British government, finally agreed a complicated federal structure for the union of their three nations. The Federation of Rhodesia and Nyasaland, also known as Central African Federation (C.A.F.), came into effect on 1st August 1953.

Right of Admission Reserved

The increasing international makeup of guests to the Falls and changing political landscape presented a delicate dilemma for Mr Tones and the Hotel's policy in relation to its services, which had largely, if not exclusively, been reserved for 'European' guests. In November 1953 Mr Tones wrote to the General Manager of the Railways asking for guidance on the issue of Livingstone's Indian community and their patronage of the Hotel's Lounge and Dining Room.

A few weeks earlier Mr Tones had asked a small visiting group of Indian guests, who had arrived at the Hotel for afternoon tea and were seated on the veranda, to relocate to seating in the garden. After much debate the group decided that they would rather leave, leading to subsequent enquiries seeking to clarify if it was the Railway's policy to discriminate on the basis of colour or race.

The incident led to the Railway Company seeking legal advice, and whilst it was confirmed that there should be no discrimination based on race or colour in the services offered by Railways, a 'Right of Admission is Reserved' notice was displayed at the entrance of the Hotel to support the Manager's right to refuse service should he feel it necessary.

Central to the decision appears to be the 'susceptibilities' of Hotel guests and that any future change in policy must be of a gradual nature. In the meantime, the Hotel Manager was empowered to exercise his discretion in the matter. Considerations revolved around visitor levels at the Hotel, the Lounge and Dining Room facilities being primarily for accommodated guests and often oversubscribed during busy periods, although it was accepted that the Hotel would have *"difficulty in continuing to evade the issue."*

Another issue arose with how the Hotel catered for the increasing numbers of African-American guests, the Railway General Manager confirming that *"after correspondence with the Division of Justice and Internal Affairs and the American Vice Consul, it was agreed to accommodate such persons subject to certain*

Study in Private Suite

provisos including the stipulation that a private suite would be allocated and meals partaken therein" (Rhodesia Railways, August 1956b).

On the 8th January 1960, as a result of Southern Rhodesia Government Notice No.32 of 1960, the Hotel officially became a multi-racial facility, open to all.

Ministers and Milk

The Federation presented new opportunities for Livingstone businesses in serving the Hotel, or so they hoped. In 1956 Hotel management correspondence shows that the Minister of Transport, following lobbying from Livingstone representatives, wrote to the Hotel enquiring *"why supplies for the Victoria Falls Hotel were purchased in Bulawayo and not locally"* (Rhodesia Railways, March 1956).

The subsequent enquiry resulted in a chain or correspondence, between the General Manager and Secretary of the Railways, the Minister's office and the Livingstone Town Clerk's office, over a period of six months on the subject of the central purchasing policy of the Catering Department, and specifically, the issue of milk. The correspondence ends with the Railway's General Manager explaining to the Ministry:

"Due consideration was given to the local tender at the time, but the contract was awarded to the Bulawayo firm because the milk supplied in Livingstone was not pasteurised. It is worthy of mention that this action was approved by the Railway Medical Officer, Livingstone [Dr William Cohen], who, after discussion with the Medical Officer of Health, agreed that local supplies were unsatisfactory." (Rhodesia Railways, August 1956a)

However the issue of the Hotel's milk supply was raised again on a national stage a few years later in a letter to the Editor of the Bulawayo Chronicle:

"I have been told that on one occasion there was a milk shortage at the Hotel and a visitor, on inquiring why powdered milk was used, was informed that the milk had to be purchased in Bulawayo as no pasteurised milk was available in Livingstone." (Bulawayo Chronicle, April 1958b)

Three Teas a Day

"The Victoria Falls Hotel, only a short walk from the falls, ...provides a level of luxury hard to match. A modern room, three teas per day(!), and lavish meals, make Victoria a place one leaves reluctantly." (Flight Magazine, 1955)

Caronia Cruises

Global cruise travel during the 1950s was dominated by the luxury first-class transatlantic RMS Caronia (known as the 'Green Goddess'), launched by Cunard White Star in 1947. Cunard introduced the first Great World Cruise in 1951, although this first tour did not stop at the Cape subsequent Caronia tours incorporated Cape Town, Port Elizabeth and Durban, allowing the predominantly American passengers to disembark and undertake specially arranged train services to the Falls.

One passenger, Mr T R Schoonover, visiting the Falls in 1952, recorded his thoughts on the Hotel in his travelogue:

"On arrival at Victoria Falls on Saturday, February 2nd, we went at once to the elegant resort hotel there and were quartered in a large high-ceiling room with private, modern bath. Found many well-to-do Englishmen and South Africans in the extensive, rambling structure, which has two storeys and no elevators, but long corridors fanning out from two lobbies... From front verandah the low rumble of the Falls can be heard and spray mist can be seen rising about a mile away.

"Dining room cool and inviting... Very strange-looking and tasting food - but good. All hot dishes are curry flavoured, fruits dead ripe - but, just try to get a piece of ice! Iced-tea is lukewarm and tepid, but moist. When guest orders, waiter dashes to kitchen and brings only one thing at a time. Took three trips to get me bacon and eggs for breakfast - once for bacon and once for each egg...

All aboard the Hotel launch

"Most of Caronia group visited Victoria Falls dressed in

bathing suits, raincoats and galoshes to withstand heavy spray at the chasm rim, opposite the falls. Returned to hotel drenched to skin and rubbers squashing water. I declined to make this trip - too muddy and slippery - but instead visited west edge and saw Devil's Gorge, which completely satisfied my taste for falls."

"Took 'Pushmobile' [rail trolley] *from huge bronze monument of Dr. Livingstone to small park above falls where the daring and the brave may risk their necks going by canoe across the rapids to an island in the middle of the on-rushing Zambesi River to view the cascades from both sides. The only safeguard against going over the falls, in case of a punctured canoe or a lost paddle, is a cable with floating oil drums attached extending from river bank to the island. It did not require too much willpower on my part to say 'No' to a suggested canoe trip...*

"Back aboard train at 3 p.m. on Sunday and headed south for Johannesburg. About 10 miles [16 km] *out we passed second special train of Caronia passengers who were following our course. Stopped and exchanged greetings for twenty minutes with our fellow travellers after four days separation."* (Schoonover, 1952)

A walk in the grounds

Early 1955 saw three parties of passengers from their Caronia cruise, some 200 in all, visiting the Falls. The two larger parties, both numbering about 65, made the trip by train; the third party of approximately 40 travelled by air. Unfortunately for those travelling by train heavy rains and flooding rather upset their schedule:

"Owing to heavy washaways... both trains were late in reaching Bulawayo, and the tourists' stay at the Falls was reduced to a minimum. The first party reached Bulawayo shortly before 11 p.m. on Wednesday, Feb 16th, and was away again within he hour. The train reached the Falls at midday the next day and left the same evening... The second train

arrived in Bulawayo shortly after midday on Thursday, Feb 17th, and left again the same evening arriving at the Falls shortly before 7 a.m. the next morning. The return trip was commenced the same evening, the tourists again being given a few hours to see the sights in and around Bulawayo on their way south." (Rhodesia Railway Magazine, March 1955)

The American tourists were still somewhat of a novelty at the Falls:

"Nearly all this happy crowd supported gay clothes and peaked caps, while their varied assortment of cameras must have clicked or whirred in a thousand different places. The lounges of the Victoria Falls Hotel resounded to merry laughter and their fascinating American 'twang,' and a crowd of well-wishers gathered on the station on both evenings to wave them goodbye." (Rhodesia Railway Magazine, April 1955b)

A further Caronia cruise in 1956 saw a smaller group of American travellers visit the Falls, with all 80 tourists travelling aboard one special train service.

"The mail train from the north pulled into the Falls Station about half-an-hour before the 'Caronia' special was due to leave. After its scheduled stop, the guard sounded his whistle, the bell went and the train slowly pulled off. One of the tourists, an elderly lady, tore out of the hotel at top speed. 'Stop the traain - stop the traain!' She screamed almost on the point of hysteria. She was positive she had missed her train-de-luxe. She had to be forcibly prevented from boarding the mail [train]. *A sympathetic South African Railways Train Manager had to reassure - and comfort - her."* (Rhodesia Railway Magazine, March 1956)

Railway Porter

Fifty Years of Service

An article published shortly after the Hotel celebrated its fiftieth anniversary detailed the Hotel's staff as one of the secrets of its success:

"The Victoria Falls bring to the Hotel thousands of guests every year; but some observers believe that the hotel brings, if not thousands, hundreds of sightseers to the Falls every year. They are not far wrong. With its quiet efficiency, its unostentatious luxury, its fine cuisine, its all-round amenities, and its moderate tariff - there is surely no other hotel in Africa of this standard with such a low tariff - the Falls Hotel is an attraction in itself. Probing into what makes the Falls Hotel 'click,' one feels that the key lies in the hotel's ubiquitous, inestimable African staff... No less than 263 Africans (directed by 33 Europeans) are employed for the Hotel's full complement of 240 guests...

"For nearly half a century most of the Africans have come from one village, Mukuni, 12 miles [19 km] from the Hotel... in Northern Rhodesia... Today 75 percent of the staff are still from Mukuni village, either of the Nuleya [Leya] or Mlozi [Lozi] tribe. Many of their fathers have worked at the Hotel and the tradition of hotel service is so strongly ingrained in Mukuni that there is a constant flow of recruits to the Hotel. Headmen and the sons of headmen themselves seek employment at the Hotel, and they are allowed special leave facilities to attend tribal councils."

The author was careful, however, to define success in terms of customer satisfaction rather than financial performance.

"For the Falls Hotel has always been run at a loss - during the last financial year the Hotel recorded a loss of £8,273. A private concern, intent on profits, could not increase the Hotel's patronage; it could raise tariffs, eliminate amenities or reduce staff, but the Rhodesia Railways, when it comes to the Falls Hotel, does not apparently think along such lines. Its continued contribution to good living away from home at a reasonable tariff must be to the administration as precious as it is to some of those who have savoured the Hotel's hospitality."

An example of the Hotel's efficient staff organisation was its handling of new arrivals from the train:

"Sometimes a train brings anything from 50 to 80 guests at a time for the Hotel. A number of the Hotel's porters are on the platform and immediately take over the luggage and line up outside the entrance to the Hotel... Meanwhile the

*guests queue up for the reception desk... As soon as a guest has completed
the necessary formalities, a bedroom boy waiting on the right is immediately
available to take over the key, claim the guest's luggage from the porters and
show the guest to his room. If you are the first in the queue, it might take you
about five minutes to be in your bedroom from the time you step off the train."*
(Aberman, 1955)

Livingstone Centenary

On 16th November 1955 a ceremony was held to commemorate the centenary of
Dr David Livingstone's first arrival at the Falls. Guests of honour at the ceremony
and staying at the Falls Hotel included Dr Hubert Wilson, Livingstone's grandson,
and Miss Dianna Livingstone-Bruce, his great grand-daughter.

End of Trolley Service

The growth of motorised transport and development of local road infrastructure
paved the way for a more flexible method of local transportation for visitors around
the Falls and the Hotel trolley system was eventually decommissioned.

*"In 1957, the Southern Rhodesia Government built a road to the Boat House,
and in December of that year the hotel replaced the hand-pushed trolley by a
service of nine-seat minibuses."* (Price, 1966)

Dr William W Cowen, the railway medical officer based at the Falls and close friend
of Mr Tones, the Hotel manager, recalled the passing of the trolley system:

*"This form of
transport had been
in used for many
years without
any denunciatory
opinion being
made, but in the
latter part of the
fifth decade the
manager of the
Hotel and the
general manager
of the railways
began to receive*

The Hotel's new minibus service

letters from guests complaining about the employment of human beings to propel the trolleys. The truth of the matter was that being 'trolley boys' was the most popular occupation of all hotel employees. The job was not nearly as physically taxing as they made out. The heavy panting was made audible in order to secure a good gratuity at the journey's end." (Cowen, 1995)

The decommissioned 45 lb (20.4 kg) rails were acquired by the Gwelo and District Light Railway Society and used to build a short two kilometre local track. One of the original trolleys, a reminder of days past, still waits under the shade of the mango trees in the Falls Hotel courtyard and offers a shady seat for quiet contemplation for today's visitors. A plaque records:

"The Victoria Falls Hotel trolley service, which operated from the Hotel to the Bridge and the Boat House, was introduced in 1920. Before this date the Hotel guests were conveyed to various points of interest by means of rickshaws. During their life the trolleys were used by some 2 million guests, and were replaced by motor coaches in December, 1957, after 37 years of romantic, yet reliable service."

Hotel For Sale?

Now a nationalised body, Rhodesia Railways management answered to the higher authority of the Ministry of Transport. In mid-1957 an internal railway memorandum recorded that the Minister of Transport, Mr Eastwood, had proposed to the Railways Board:

"It might be advantageous for the Railways to take over the Beit Trustees' share of the capital or, in view of the provision in the lease, that the Railways should take over the undertaking at the capital cost less the amount of depreciation. The Railways could then subsequently sell the building to outside interests which would no doubt yield a substantial capital return to the Railways." (Rhodesia Railways, July 1957)

The Beit Trust held 70,204 shares in the Victoria Falls Hotel Company, a thirty-five percent stake, with the remainder of the 200,000 shares owned by the Railway Company. In November 1957 the Rhodesia Railways Board recorded:

"They could see no difficulty in the matter of the Railways obtaining ownership of the Victoria Falls Hotel and its possible resale subsequently to private enterprise... provided that it was ensured that the purchasers would be able and willing to maintain the existing high standard of the Hotel. With this object

The train departs

*in view and in order also to ensure that the maximum price would be realised
they felt that world-wide tenders should be called for. They were emphatically
of the opinion that no offer under £500,000 should be entertained. In addition, it
was considered that the Beit Trustees should be apprised of the reason for the
Railways acquiring ownership."* (Rhodesia Railways, November 1957)

Competition was also on the horizon, with the Northern Rhodesia Government
announcing in 1957 the lease of a specially selected site, just above the Falls on
the northern bank, for the development of a luxury 200 bedroom hotel and casino.
News of the potential sale of the Hotel, now regarded a 'national asset,' reached
the press in April 1958, with the Minister confirming to the Bulawayo Chronicle that
disposal of the Hotel was being considered, whilst denying that a deal had already
been done with an American financier.

*"The Minister of Transport Mr Eastwood yesterday denied categorically that
the Federal Government planned to sell the Victoria Falls Hotel to an American
financier. Mr Eastwood said he had nothing to add to his statement of last
week, in which he said the possibility of selling the Hotel was being considered."*
(Bulawayo Chronicle, April 1958a)

A South African millionaire with American business interests, Mr Schlesinger, was
named in press reports as looking to develop a 'drink-and-gamble-round-the-clock
hotel on the south or north bank of the river.' Months passed before the Minister
was again called to clarify the future of the Hotel.

*"The Minister of Transport, Mr Eastwood, said yesterday that there was no
question of the Federal Government disposing of the Victoria Falls Hotel
'precipitately' or without reference to all interested parties."* (Bulawayo
Chronicle, September 1958)

The Beit Trustees subsequently agreed to the sale of their shareholding as proposed, and in early 1959 it was confirmed at the annual Ordinary General Meeting of the Victoria Falls Hotel Company Ltd that *"the Beit Trust's shares were accordingly acquired in Jan, 1959, for the sum of £74,361"* (Victoria Falls Hotel Ltd, 1959).

Following notification from the Railways Company as to the purchase of the Beit Trust's shareholding in January 1959, the Ministry of Transport wrote to the Railway Board confirming that *"the possibility of an advantageous sale of the Victoria Falls Hotel to a suitable purchaser should be investigated."* It appears the Administration itself even considered the purchase of the Hotel.

"In the course of this discussion the Minister stated that if the Railways could earn a reasonable return on the money which might be obtained from the sale of the Hotel, he would have no objection to the retention of the Hotel by the Administration. He stated that he regarded a sum of £750,000 as a reasonable assessment of what would be obtained from the sale of the Hotel buildings plus, say £50,000 for the furnishings, stock and equipment." (Rhodesia Railways, January 1959)

The Ministry of Transport also later confirmed to the Railways Board:

"Amongst the points to be kept in mind in dealing with this subject are undertakings given publicly by the Minister to the effect that proposals for purchase would be publicly invited, that sale would not be effected precipitately or secretly, and that before arriving at a final decision all interested parties would be consulted on questions such as the future of the Victoria Falls Hotel staff etc; in addition the Minister may wish to consult the Northern and Southern Governments" (Rhodesia Railways, June 1959a).

Cruise trip departs

Reviewing Resources

In the early days of the Hotel many of the support staff lived and commuted from Mukuni Village on the north side of the river. By the fifties the Hotel employed around 250 African staff, levels deemed high but necessary on account of the layout and of the Hotel. Increasingly staff, who were employed by the Railway Company, were based in the growing African township on the south bank, which would become known as Chinotimba.

With increased focus on the operational performance of the Hotel, the Management turned its attention to one of its greatest assets - the staff.

"As regards African staff, both the Catering Superintendent and the Hotel Manager have made every effort to reduce the numbers employed, but it must be remembered that the Hotel is not modern in construction and is, in fact, rambling and difficult to control. Continuous reductions in the number of staff have been made over a period of years, even to the extent of reducing the 'service' in the Hotel. The Catering Superintendent hopes to reduce the number of African staff to 200, and might be able to reduce the number further by introducing telephones in each bedroom and changing the existing methods of meeting visitor's room requirements. This matter is under examination." (Rhodesia Railways, June 1959b)

Dr Cowen records a significant milestone for the Hotel's African employees.

"African nationalism was developing in the three territories, though it is doubtful if it influenced the agitation by employees at the Victoria Falls Hotel to demand the right to wear tackies (a name given to canvas shoes with rubber soles). I personally agreed with their reasonable request, which was eventually granted. Apart from the waiters, none of the African workers at the Hotel had shoes included in their uniforms; they were expected to pad silently along the corridors and in the rooms barefooted." (Cowen, 1995)

Slipping Standards

With the immediate future of the Hotel still unresolved the Railway Board, now sole owners of the Hotel, declared *"that the* [Victoria Falls Hotel] *Company would continue in existence, and ...directed that expenditure on maintenance should be restricted, but that there should be no reduction in the service at the Hotel"* (Rhodesia Railways, October 1958).

A memorandum from the General Manager to the Railway Board in January 1959, however, raised concerns over the impact of these economies on the standard of services at the Hotel:

"Since the first advice of the possible sale of the Victoria Falls Hotel was received, expenditure has been curtailed on items of furniture, equipment, linen, etc. and maintenance of the building, furnishing and equipment has been reduced to a minimum. Additionally, in order to improve the net revenue positions, economies have been effected in other directions. It has been apparent for some time that this policy has had the effect of reducing the high standard previously maintained by the Hotel and, whilst I realise that it was not the Board's intention that standards should be lowered, it is obvious that any general instruction regarding economy and the reduction of maintenance expenditure is bound to have some effect on standards."

Having discussed the matter with the Hotel Manager, the General Manager confirmed:

"Instructions have now been issued for certain essential maintenance to be done at once and for staff changes calculated to improve the standards of service. As you are aware, there have been several complaints in recent months of the facilities offered by the Hotel, and when the Minister was in my office recently these were mentioned. The Minister was informed that some of the staff difficulties were due to uncertainty regarding the future of the Hotel and that a final decision, at an early date, on whether a sale was to be effected, would enable us to plan accordingly." (Rhodesia Railways, January 1959)

One such complaint had come from a Mr Graylin via the Ministry of Transport. In reply in June 1958, the Railway Secretary confirmed that a detailed investigation of the matter had been carried out.

"At the time Mr Graylin was staying at the Hotel, decorators had been, and still were, working on the repainting of the lounges, writing room, corridors and bedrooms... It is agreed that some of the furniture is showing slight wear, having been in use since the Royal Visit in 1947, but, generally speaking, suites are in good condition. It is agreed that work on the lines mentioned and in other ways, i.e. improved telephone facilities throughout the Hotel, are most necessary, but it is doubtful whether the cost involved would be recouped if and when the Hotel is sold to private enterprise." (Rhodesia Railways, June 1958)

A Rambling Edifice

Major Wilfred Theodore Blake, a well known British aviator and travel writer, visited the Federation during the late 1950s, publishing a book of his travels.

"We duly arrived at the Victoria Falls Hotel, a large and rambling edifice badly planned from nearly ever point of view. When we were there twenty-five years ago, we were told the architect had committed suicide and I am not surprised! Since then it has been enlarged and complicated. Our room was at the end of one of the wings and to get from it to our car parked outside the entrance to the hotel took 389 paces. There was no telephone in the bedroom and in order to communicate with the outside world we had to walk about 250 paces to the telephone box." (Blake, 1960)

The Hotel management fully recognised that the Hotel was in need of substantial modernisation in regard to air-conditioning and telephone services, which were still only provided in a limited number of rooms.

"Certain rooms, but not all, are equipped with internal service telephones. Guests who wish to make calls to places outside the Hotel, via the Livingstone telephone exchange, have to use the Public call box. Here again the Hotel is antiquated and many complaints have been received regarding the difficulty in communicating with the outside world." (Rhodesia Railways, April 1960)

A year later the Vice Chairman of the Railway Company himself echoed concerns

"The Hotel buildings are in the main part old and do not lend themselves readily to economical management. This has handicapped the Railways in making a success of the Hotel either as a Railway investment or as a

Telephone service in one of the luxury suites

tourist amenity. In addition uncertainty regarding the future of the Hotel has resulted in a degree of 'Standstill' in the Railways' management of it and put a stop to plans for improvements and development. The position now is that the Hotel is not only bringing the Railways a disproportionately small return on its investment but it is also bringing the Railways undesirable publicity, added to which there is growing pressure from tourist organisations for the standards of accommodation and service at the Hotel to be raised to the level expected by moneyed tourists." (Rhodesia Railways, March 1961)

Regimental Roots

Blake goes on to record an interesting encounter with a member of the Hotel staff.

"Whilst in the lounge of the Victoria Falls Hotel I was struck by the fact that one of the African waiters spoke perfect English though with a strong Scotch accent. I assumed because of this he came from Nyasaland, but on asking him if this was so, much to my surprise, he replied; 'No I come from Edinburgh. I was born at 80 Princes Street.' His story is that his name is MacTavish and that his father had served in the Black Watch [3rd Battalion, Royal Regiment of Scotland]. *He went to school in Edinburgh and then followed in his father's footsteps, serving in the Black Watch for a number of years before coming out to Africa."* (Blake, 1960)

Flying the Flag

Railway Company correspondence reveals debate over the continued flying of the British Union Flag at the Hotel and Falls Station.

"I am directed to invite your attention to the fact that during a recent visit to the Victoria Falls, the Minister of Home Affairs noticed that tattered Union Jacks were being flown at the Hotel and at the station which, he felt, were not a good advertisement to show, particularly in a tourist centre. In drawing attention to this matter... it might be desirable to fly the Federal Flag in addition to the Union Jack in a good state of repair. As the Railways are doubtless aware, where both flags are flown, the Union Jack will naturally be on the right." (Rhodesia Railways, June 1959a)

In response the Railways General Manager replied that he did *"not think it is necessary to fly flags daily at any station, and... I propose to discontinue the practice, except of course on... special occasions."*

"As regards the Federal Flag, it does not appear, at any rate up to the present, to be general practice to fly it as well as the Union Jack on Federal Government buildings, and I feel it is perhaps hardly necessary." (Rhodesia Railways, August 1959)

Fewer Visitors

During the 1950s the Hotel's occupancy averaged around 20,000 guest-nights a year. Figures showed that there was a substantial increase in the number of visitors arriving from the United States, but a decline in the numbers coming from the United Kingdom.

"During the year ending June last, visitors staying at the Victoria Falls Hotel dropped to 17,864 - against 19,314 for the previous year. The annual report of Rhodesia Railways, published yesterday, says the Hotel was affected by economic conditions in the Federation last year. The number of meals served in the Hotel during the year dropped to 150,007 from 153,754 the year before." (Bulawayo Chronicle, May 1959)

A Question of Land

Sale of the Hotel to a third party depended on the removal of restrictive conditions in the land title deeds. Action was taken to consolidate the two pieces of land on which the Hotel was sited, *"with the intention of then applying for the excision of the restrictive conditions in the land titles"* (Rhodesia Railways, June 1959b). In March 1960 the Secretary for Local Government finally clarified the situation regarding the lease of the Railway Reserve land to the Hotel:

"Reference is made to... previous correspondence regarding your request that the existing Title Deed should be freed of the restrictive clause to enable you to dispose of the Hotel property, should it be desired. Government has given careful consideration to this request but regrets that it cannot be granted." (Rhodesia Railways, March 1960)

This ruling effectively prevented any such sale to a third party. Initially it was suggested that the Railway Company might agree to transferring the site, and Hotel, back to the Government free of cost, or alternatively pay the current market value of the land for full and clear title. However this then raised another issue, with the Secretary also subsequently confirming continuing Government policy not to allow any private land ownership at the Falls.

A Change of Plan

Unable to dispose of the Hotel, it was decided that *"the Victoria Falls Hotel Company Limited be dissolved on the 30th June 1961"* (Rhodesia Railways, March 1961), with the Hotel reverting to the direct control of the Rhodesia Railways, and preparations made to get the Hotel into shape to be leased as a viable operational concern.

The Victoria Falls Hotel Management Committee, including the Hotel Manager and various other Rhodesia Railways appointed members, was established to oversee the management of the Hotel, reporting directly to the Rhodesia Railways Board. The Hotel's management was uncoupled from the Catering Department of the Railway Company, and the manager empowered to control purchases direct from local suppliers. A new accounting system was also introduced, designed to present a clearer picture of the Hotel's operating position, which would no longer be supplemented or supported by Railway Company funding.

Mr Peter Patrick Alexander Webster was promoted as the Hotel's new General Manager on 1st July 1961 following the transfer of Mr Tones to the Catering Administrative Office in Bulawayo. Mr Webster, who had originally joined the Hotel's Food and Beverages staff in 1947 and become Assistant Manager under Mr Tones, took over responsibility for an operation suffering from years of restricted investment and inherited a comprehensive list of capital improvements *"considered essential in order to keep the Hotel in operation as a first class establishment"* (Rhodesia Railways, April 1964). Funding, however, was limited and works had to be prioritised and phased over several years.

The Rainbow Room

One of the first improvements identified by Mr Webster was the provision of a new cocktail bar, converted from a section of the main lounge. The previous cocktail bar being described as *"too small for a hotel of this size, is in dilapidated condition and enjoys no outlook. The new bar will provide a view of the Bridge, will accommodate four times the number of people, and in addition will be fully air-conditioned and elegantly furnished"* (Rhodesia Railways, November 1961).

The works were commissioned in late 1961 and undertaken between January and March 1962 at a cost of £8,000. The Rainbow Room was officially opened on 1st April 1962 and was the first fully air-conditioned cocktail bar in the country. Also in 1962 the private Hammerhead suites were upgraded to luxury air-conditioned suites.

The new Rainbow Room bar

"'Without a reasonable and up-to-date hotel at the Victoria Falls there is no doubt that tourist traffic would suffer,' said Mr J H Allen, General Manager, Rhodesia Railways, speaking at the opening of the Rainbow Room. 'I think we may face a very formidable competitor in the next couple of years,' he said, 'but our opinion is that there will still be need for a hotel of the standard of this one. The new Rainbow Room is a practical demonstration of our faith in the future of the Hotel and an increasing tourist trade.'" (Rhodesia Railway Magazine, June 1962)

Subsequent extensions to the public rooms resulted in the enclosing of the front veranda and masking of the Hotel's original facade and architectural features.

Conferences and Cocktails

The Hotel was a popular venue for professional conferences, and hosted no fewer than six major conferences over two months in 1961, catering for several hundred delegates at a time.

"During the period of some eight to ten weeks extending well into June, the Victoria Falls Hotel entertained the delegates to no fewer than five national conventions and, in one instance, one of a fully international character. The number of guests ran into the thousand bracket - and more - and they came

from all parts of Southern Africa and from more than a dozen different overseas countries."

The Hotel's Chief Chef, Mr Michael Vlotman, had developed a significant reputation for his skills over eighteen years of service at the Hotel.

"For the 'break up party' of the Association of Municipal Electrical Undertakings the Victoria Falls Hotel served a lavish buffet supper to over 400 delegates and their guests. This repast, arranged by Chief Chef, Mike Vlotman, has as its piece-de-resistance whole Canadian salmon ready to be sliced, while the variety of meats included boar's head, chaudfroid of chicken, glazed hams, turkey, rare baron of beef, chicken en aspic, galantines of chicken, old English pork pies, and veal pies.

"At the special request of the National Federation of Business and Professional Women of Rhodesia and Nyasaland, a banquet was arranged which was lifted quite out of the ordinary by its all-Rhodesian theme. The menu included monkey-nut soup, Zambesi Bream and braised venison, much to the delight of the overseas visitors, while the tables were gay with Rhodesian flowers and with menus on which the Rhodesian emblem, the flame lily, had been hand painted by members of the Livingstone Club." (Rhodesia Railways Magazine, July 1961).

A 1963 Hotel wine list and drinks menu shows imaginatively named cocktails inspired from the local landscape, with alcoholic cocktail delights such as the 'Big Tree,' 'Boiling Pot,' 'Devil's Cataract,' 'Knife Edge,' 'Lunar Rainbow' and 'Palm Grove.' Non-alcoholic cocktails included 'Eve's Footprint,' 'Kandahar Monkey,' 'Pink Elephant,' 'Silent Pool' and 'Falls Spray.'

Chief Chef Mr Vlotman tempts guests with his creations

Beware Baboons

Living with the local wildlife has always been part of the charm, and challenge, of the Falls. The behaviour of baboons and vervet monkeys in particular presenting a never ending challenge to a succession of managers at the Hotel.

"Manager Peter Webster is a charming young Boniface with a wholesome respect for the old ways of gracious living. In fact, Mr Webster is so concerned about the comfort of his guests that he has even placed signs in the garden and on the terraces which read: 'Warning - Do not feed or approach too close to baboons in this area.' Troops of these simians that inhabit the trees, roofs and - on occasion - even the rooms of the Victoria Falls Hotel can become not only contemptuous but downright obstreperous at any demonstration of undue familiarity. They have been known to snatch cakes out of the hands of ladies at tea time." (Cosmopolitan, 1962)

Dr Cowen, the railway medical officer based in Livingstone and who held surgeries at the Hotel for staff and guests during the 1950s recalled:

"Another troupe of baboons lived in the bush near the front of the Hotel and visitors having their afternoon tea on the veranda would be surprised by baboons coming up to snatch cakes from their tables. Africans were

Tea in the grounds

specially employed to keep the baboons and monkeys away from the Hotel
by brandishing large poles to beat them off. In fact 'baboon operative' was an
officially-designated grade of worker in the railways." (Cowen, 1995)

The Canadian travel writer Willard Price noted more cautiously:

"Lest the luxury hotel fool anyone into supposing that he is as safe as in his
own town, the sign 'All wild animals are dangerous' confronts him just where the
path across the hotel lawn enters the woods. This warning applies even to the
baboons, which crowd curiously around the swimming pool to watch bathers.
They are usually docile but some old rogues are mean. Lion spoor is found near
the kitchen door and elephants knock down the telephone wires." (Price, 1962)

Ripples at the Landing Stage

In addition to the ongoing restructuring and redevelopments at the Hotel, there
were decisions to be made on the future of the Hotel's transport services. By 1963
the Hotel's buses and launches were reaching the end of their operational life-
spans, and in order to avoid the expenditure of replacement it was decided to end
the internal operation of the Hotel's boat and minibus services.

In the early 1960s the Falls Hotel had looked at expanding its facilities and services
at the Boat House and Landing Stage. The site, a short distance upstream from the
Falls, was leased by the Railway Company on behalf of the Hotel. Over the years
the facilities had developed to include a boat shed, launch slipway and an open-air
tearoom for waiting passengers, serving 'the best tea and cream buns in the Falls.'
In the early sixties the Hotel management seriously considered expanding the site
into a fully-fledged visitor restaurant with car-parking facilities. An internal Hotel
report in 1963 concluded:

"After considering very carefully the provision of a restaurant at the boat house
on the south bank of the Zambezi it was decided, that in view of the shortage
of capital funds together with the fact that we were only able to obtain a very
restricted liquor licence, the project should be abandoned." (Victoria Falls Hotel
Management Committee, March 1963)

Hotel management committee reports recorded that numerous delays were
encountered in negotiations over the sublease of the Landing Stage site, and
that during these delays, the launches and Boat House were totally destroyed
by a freak fire. Documents do not detail the cause of the fire and the site was
abandoned. The Railway Company duly terminated the leases for the site and also

The Hotel boathouse on the river

the picnic-site on Kandahar Island, bringing to an end the Hotel's long association operating river launches and tours.

Requiring an immediate replacement for their launch services, the Hotel management turned to Livingstone based Greenway Launches & Taxi Services, operated by Mr A S Sussens from the north bank, the only operator with the capacity to deliver an adequate service for the Hotel. Whilst appreciating Mr Sussens cooperation in ensuring that the Hotel suffered no disruption to its launch services for its guests, the Hotel Management soon after decided it unwise to pass all their clientele to a single operator, preferring to share their business among two or more companies and encouraging some healthy competition.

Contract Competition

The Falls Hotel management committee eventually determined that the Hotel would *"benefit by allowing private enterprise to take over the launch services, under certain safeguards to the Management, on the understanding that the Hotel would be the sole booking agent for all trips, on a 10% commission basis"* (Victoria Falls Hotel Management Committee, March 1963).

The contract for the operation of the Hotel's vehicle transfers and boat tours was included in an invitation to private companies which appeared in the Livingstone Mail in September 1963. The call for tender appears to have sparked a scramble between Livingstone businesses, none of which appeared to have the existing capacity or quality of services the Hotel required. Partnerships were made, and broken, new companies formed and investors sought, all in the chase to land the Hotel's business.

Mr Harry Sossen, a businessman of some standing in Livingstone and manager of the Victoria Falls Garage on the south bank, originally agreed a partnership with the established Zambezi Safaris company, based on the southern bank and operated by Mr Jocelyn. However they were quickly to part company, for reasons unknown, with Mr Sossen setting himself up in the boating business on the north bank, and even going as far as to purchase the launches and buses necessary for the contract. Zambezi Safaris found themselves another financial investor, this time from Bulawayo, and together with several other companies, submitted proposals.

In 1964 the Hotel's transport and booking desk services were contracted to the United Touring Company, who were to exclusively manage and operate the Hotel's river cruises and local tours for many years. The Hotel's landing stage site was abandoned and reclaimed by nature, whilst new commercial jetty sites were developed further upstream, leased to a new wave of tour operators.

Today the site of the old Landing Stage can still be located along Zambezi Drive, with a series of steps down the riverbank. Only recently, in 2014, local resident Mr Godwill Ruona's sharp eyes happened to spot something exposed in the receding water, and pulled out of the mud a small brass plaque reading 'DIANA - 16 passengers.' Mr Ruona has presented the name plate to the Jafuta Heritage Centre (located at the Elephant's Walk Shopping Village, Victoria Falls) for future display.

Ready to depart

Changing Rooms and Roles

In an internal report to the Hotel's Management Committee in March 1963, Mr Webster reviewed progress against a comprehensive list of maintenance issues and development requirements.

The exterior of the Hotel was one of the first issues tackled, the complete exterior needing repainting. Work had started in 1961 and was phased over several years. One of the most urgent priorities was to repair the Hotel's leaking roof, described as being in *"very poor condition* [and] *leaking in many places with the result that part of the paintwork inside the hotel was in a shabby condition."*

Redecoration of bedrooms received priority once the roof had been repaired. The management were faced with the problem of walls which were *"prone to cracking due to the variations in temperature. All attempts in the past to re-plaster and re-decorate had failed to provide a lasting solution to this problem."*

An experiment was conducted in one of the rooms subject to cracks with a new type of 'elasticated' wallpaper. This proved successful and four other rooms were selected for the same treatment. *"It is hoped to continue a steady programme of redecoration in this manner until all the bedrooms with this type of wall have been done."*

The lack of dancing space had always been a shortcoming at the Hotel. *"It was decided... to provide a dance floor in the existing dining room, as near the same level of the existing*

Bedroom with en-suite bathroom

Dinner dancing, with Mr Webster seated at head of table

dining room floor as possible so that the area could also be used as dining space when necessary."

A Rhodesian teak wood parquet dance floor was laid in the early sixties, Mr Webster reporting: *"The dance floor has been in use for several months and has proved a big attraction, particularly to the Livingstone residents. Dinner/dances are now possible, and live music is provided on a Saturday night until midnight, during which the à la carte menu is available."*

Conversely to the lack of space on the ground floor, the Summer Parlour, described as *"a very large room situated above the main lounge, for which the manager was unable to find any other use because of the unattractive approach to it,"* was to double as a games room *"if and when required, but further consideration should be given to its possible conversion to suites, or some useful purpose."*

Despite having his hands full the Manager appeared confident *"that the improvements so far introduced at the Hotel have had marked effect upon the clientele and as this becomes more widely known there would appear to be no reason why the present favourable trends should not continue to develop"* (Rhodesia Railways, March 1963).

In early 1963 Mr Webster was transferred back to the Catering Department Head

Office in Bulawayo, initially covering for Mr Tones as Catering Administrative Officer, who was himself covering for Mr Shinn, the Chief Catering Officer, and both of who were shortly due to retire. As a temporary measure Mr W Johnstone was appointed Acting Manager at the Hotel, with Mr Webster overseeing the role from Bulawayo (Rhodesia Railways, February 1963).

Mr Johnstone, however, was the Senior Stocktaker at Head Office, and apparently did not desire the permanent post of Hotel Manager. At the same time the Management Board were reluctant to appoint a new manager whilst the uncertain operating status of the Hotel continued, with the transition to being managed independently from the Catering Department proving rather problematic (Rhodesia Railways, May 1963).

Now in a more senior role at Head Office, Mr Webster was appointed to the Hotel Management Board committee. At their 11th meeting, held in May 1963, Mr Webster successfully recommended the dropping of the off-season reduced tariff and the adoption of a universal rate - whilst at the same time it was agreed to introduce a higher rate during the Christmas, Easter and public holiday periods, when the Hotel's accommodation 'could be sold over and over' (Rhodesia Railways, May 1963).

Federation Folly

Increasing African nationalism, particularly in Northern Rhodesia and Nyasaland, persuaded Britain to agree to the organised dissolution of the Federation. The 'break-up' negotiations, known as the Central Africa Conference, involving delegates from five governments, were hosted in the Pullman Suite at the Hotel over several days in July 1963. The Federation was officially dissolved on the 31st December 1963.

> *"Preparations for the recent conference at the Victoria Falls Hotel to discuss the dissolution of the Federation proved to be an undertaking of some magnitude. There were a hundred and one things to be done. Dozens of extra telephones had to be installed; telex machines accommodated and connected up to many parts of Southern Africa as well as overseas; press and additional conference rooms prepared; and above all, the strictest security measures introduced. One of the minor items of these security arrangements was the fitting of locks to all outside doors - doors with locks that had not been used for more years than anyone could remember. They even fitted a new lock to the outside door of the Chapel wing."* (Rhodesia Railways Magazine, August 1963)

Call the Consultant

In mid-1963 the Rhodesia Railways Board contracted a specialist consultant, Mr Schefftel, to review the operational performance of the Hotel. The scope of the investigations were specifically identified as to *"whether the Hotel can be operated on a profitable basis under the existing form of organisation"* - with minimal or no capital expenditure - or *"whether the Hotel can be operated more profitably and efficiently in any other way."*

In August Mr Schefftel presented his report, having reviewed the Hotel's accounting and administrative systems and performance. His first observation was that the Hotel was suffering from a huge salary burden, staff wages and associated payments absorbing approximately fifty percent of its operational income. Mr Schefftel felt that *"this alone makes it quite impossible for the Hotel to operate on a paying basis."*

Attention to the grounds was felt to be *"of prime importance as the Hotel should not only be a sight-seeing headquarters for the Falls, but should also be a holiday resort in its own right."*

He went on to state *"the Hotel grounds... at present cannot by any means be considered a pleasure-giving medium. The surrounds of the Hotel were once world-famous and reputedly a paradise. No time should be lost in restoring them."*

The bar in the Rainbow Room

Mr Schefftel felt that improvements to the buildings were a second priority as *"with the exception of the kitchen and store rooms, the Hotel was in reasonable shape."* In regard to the bigger picture of the Hotel's management and operation, Mr Schefftel recorded:

"It is quite probable that private enterprise would operate the Hotel more profitably than is done at present for one very important reason. It would not be fettered with crippling wage legislation... Should some way be found eventually to lease the Hotel to private enterprise under satisfactory terms and conditions, it is of utmost importance that the high standard at present achieved should be maintained. There is no doubt whatsoever that it would be of considerable advantage to all concerned if a method could be found to divorce the directing and the management of the Hotel from the Railways Administration."

Aviation arrivals for the first time overtook those travelling by rail, making the Central African Airways one of the Hotel's largest customers. Mr Schefftel warned that *"as the majority of visitors arrive by air the future of Livingstone Airport must be of prime importance to the Hotel. Should the political situation deteriorate insofar as depriving the Hotel of its 'air' tourists, the development of the Victoria Falls [air] strip will have to be seriously considered"* (Rhodesia Railways, August 1964).

Mr Schefftel concluded: *"The thought that the Hotel is a 'White Elephant' should be dispelled in the minds of all concerned with it. It is not in the best interests of Southern Rhodesia to give visitors the impression of 'no confidence.' A new out-look and a new set-up are essential for the future of the Hotel"* (Rhodesia Railways, August 1964).

The Mysterious Case of the Mysterious Case

In mid-March 1964 the Hotel had a spring clean and handed over to the local police some 20 year's accumulation of unclaimed property, including a large leather trunk with no travel labels, a big brass lock and the name 'J Heggen.'

"The locks were forced open and inside were found the complete summer and winter uniforms of a First Officer of the British Merchant Navy. There were also a seaman's passport, a membership card for the Seamen & Navigating Officers' Union and a British wartime ration book, all in the name of James Heggen; vital documents their owner would hardly travel without... and, wrapped around his shoes, were copies of the London Evening News, dated December 1942.

"Diligently the local police undertook the necessary enquiries to find Heggen,

from dusty files that were now some twenty years old, but there was no Heggen registered in the Hotel records and no-one knew how the trunk had got there... His curiosity ablaze, the policeman wrote to the Chief of Cheshire Constabulary - the country of Heggen's last known address. The Cheshire Constabulary succeeded in locating Heggen's wife, as well as the master of Heggen's last ship, and at last the loose jigsaw puzzle pieces began to form a picture.

"James Heggen had been a First Officer with the Blue Star Line from the day he joined the Merchant Service in the 1920s. Towards the end of 1942 he was ordered to take up duties immediately as First Office aboard the S.S. Dafila of the British Continental Steamship Company... First Officer Heggen was onboard when the S.S. Dafila sailed into the Mediterranean in 1943. Off the Libyan coast, she was sunk by an enemy submarine attack. The master of the ship was on the bridge with Heggen at the time of the attack and witnessed Heggen's death from shrapnel wounds." (Kondor, 1990)

The trunk was returned to Mrs Heggen, without it ever being established exactly how it came to end up in the Hotel's lost property collection.

Management Merry-go-round

Mr Harry Rugg was appointed Manager in May 1964. Mr Rugg remained with the Hotel for only six months, leaving at the end of October 1964 on transfer to Salisbury. Mr Webster was subsequently transferred back to the Hotel, the only person to have held the post twice (Rhodesia Railways Magazine, December 1964).

Independence Issues

After the collapse of the Federation of Rhodesia and Nyasaland in 1963, Northern Rhodesia was granted independence on 24th October 1964, becoming the Republic of Zambia. Earlier in the same year Nyasaland also gained independence as the Republic of Malawi. South of the river the momentum for independent majority rule in Southern Rhodesia was also growing. However, against rising calls for democratic majority rule, the white-minority government led by Ian Smith made a Unilateral Declaration of Independence (U.D.I.) on 11th November 1965. Smith made the Declaration after days of tense negotiations with British Prime Minister Harold Wilson, who was only prepared to permit independence on the basis of giving the black majority population a fair share of power. The British Government, Commonwealth, and United Nations condemned the move as illegal, leaving Rhodesia unrecognised by the international community.

Grounds for Improvement

Having addressed many of the maintenance shortcomings to the Hotel's buildings in the previous few years, attention turned to the grounds surrounding the Hotel. The grounds were largely bare and undeveloped, with footpaths demarcated by lines of whitewashed stones running off into the bush. The Entrance Courtyard, between the Railway Station and Hotel, was improved with a new layout of roads, parking and gardens. Mr Webster reported:

"The question of patrons being able to drive right up to the main foyer and deposit the passengers had long been a bone of contention, especially in the rainy season. The provision of a new access road has overcome this and has done much to provide a more attractive approach to the Hotel." (Rhodesia Railways, March 1963)

The access road to the Hotel was named Mallet Drive after Mr Mallet, the first Manager of the Hotel employed under the Railway Company. The 'unsightly' garages located in the parking area and established for the Royal Visit in 1947 had been *"demolished as soon as possible after the new management took over"* (Rhodesia Railways, March 1963).

On 1st December 1965 the Hotel hosted an invited group of about a hundred Livingstone and Victoria Falls residents for a garden party. Mr Trevor Wright, General Manager of the Railway Company announced a £40,000 improvement plan for the grounds and outdoor facilities, to commence early in 1966 and finish mid-year (Rhodesia Railways Magazine, January 1965).

Arrival at the Hotel

The front reception area, between the Railway Station and Hotel, was identified as needing 'horticultural attention,' with the removal of some of the overgrown mango trees. Rock gardens with aloes were suggested for the car park, which was to be resurfaced with tarmac, including up to the rear entrance to the Hotel.

The upper terrace was developed, with retaining walls and side steps running down to a large patio area, and open lawns extending towards the gorge. Even the Chairman of the Rhodesia Railways Board invested time in discussions on the subject of top soil depth and type of grass to be provided (Rhodesia Railways, March 1965).

Long-planned redevelopment work to the swimming pool was undertaken. The surrounding walls were removed and the changing rooms and toilets relocated. A refreshment kiosk was also provided to serve guests at the swimming pool. Two floodlit all-weather tennis courts were developed on the site of the old bowling green, which had been established in 1948. A replacement bowling green was created between the south hammerhead wing and the tennis courts.

Remodelling and planting of the gardens was planned to commence in early December 1964, with an estimated water requirement of 22,600 gallons (102,742 litres) per acre per week, over a total area of 12 acres (4.8 hectares), all of which was supplied and paid for by the gallon (Rhodesia Railways, October 1964).

Tea on the Veranda

Upgrading Guest Services

In 1965 several new redevelopments were being planned to the interior of the Hotel and undertaken with local company Gardini & Sons as builders and Aristotelous & Co Ltd providing furniture and fittings. Architectural details were provided by the Railway Company. The works were started in October 1965 and budgeted at just over £12,000, with the conversion of new family suites a key element of the developments.

The Reception Hall of the Hotel was modernised, with *"the provision of a porter's counter and luggage room, a reception Manager's Office, accommodation for United Touring Company, and an enlarged shop,"* in addition to the existing facilities which included a banking desk operated by Barclay's Bank (Rhodesia Railways, November 1964).

"Work in the foyer was completed early in June, and the first impression one gets of the hotel's facilities is now one of complete modernity and efficiency. The new reception, accounts and porter's desks are matched by the smart appearance of the Bank and two large counters serving the airways. The assistant manager is readily available in a glass-fronted office, opposite which is a de-luxe shop fitted with wall to wall carpeting which will offer all those items a guest expects to be on sale at a luxury hotel." (Rhodesia Railways Magazine, July 1966)

New arrivals check-in at the Hotel Reception

A ladies hairdressing salon was developed through the conversion of a housekeeper's room and linen cupboard on the ground floor at the north end of the west wing.

"Those people who have not been to the Victoria Falls Hotel for a couple of years will see many improvements which include a well patronised shop in the foyer and a modern hairdressing salon which provides an extremely popular facility for hotel guests and Victoria Falls residents alike." (Rhodesia Railways Magazine, April 1967)

The development of further family suites, reflecting the increasing number of family visitors, was achieved through the conversion of the old writing room, ladies changing room and managers suite into two family suites and two bedrooms with bathrooms.

In response to rising numbers of visitors 1967 saw further modernisations at the Hotel, including the installation of air-conditioning in more of the Hotel's rooms.

Entertainment for the Masses

Despite the return of border formalities for Livingstone residents the Hotel was still a popular venue for a good night out.

"It was a bumper New Year's Eve at the Victoria Falls Hotel when some 650 people thronged the main lounge and verandas to see the Old Year out and the New Year in. Customs barriers certainly did not seem to have deterred the many merrymakers who had come over from Livingstone for celebrations. A new band is now in attendance at the hotel and is proving very popular. Known as the 'Rainbow Trio', it was started by Mr Rob Webb, who was transferred to Livingstone some four months ago as a clerk in the Reservations Office." (Rhodesia Railways Magazine, February 1965)

The 'Rainbow Trio' band proved to be a popular new attraction at the Hotel's weekend dances.

"The 'Rainbow Trio' band... was kept busy over Easter and delighted the large crowds with its excellent rhythm for ballroom and Latin-American dances which seemed greatly preferred to the modern 'swing' music. The band was photographed by a TV team but, unfortunately, with no television in this area, the members were unable to see themselves in action." (Rhodesia Railways Magazine, June 1965).

Fashion show

Fashion Mecca

The latest global fashions came to the Falls Hotel in October 1965.

"The highlight of the month at the Victoria Falls Hotel in October was an exhibition of furs and jewellery presented by a team of top South African models. It brought an atmosphere of international sophistication to the scene with a display of a kind never before seen in Rhodesia. The display was the culmination of months of preparation by Mr Dennis Erwin, a Livingstone business man, whose idea is to make Victoria Falls 'the mecca of fashion' in Southern Africa. Many wealthy tourists by-pass Bulawayo and Johannesburg, he says, and he feels that in the quiet, restful atmosphere of the Victoria Falls Hotel they can make their choice of the truly African products in the world of fashion." (Rhodesia Railways Magazine, December 1965)

Starring Roles

The Railway Company staff magazine recorded staff changes and events at the Falls Hotel, with Christmas and New Year always a busy time of year.

"The whole Victoria Falls village had a most enjoyable Christmas and New Year break, according to all accounts, and the children's Christmas Party at the Recreation Club was a great success, with Father Christmas arriving by

Poolside fun

air. The station staff, however, had a busy time for, in addition to the usual heavy quota of general goods, it handled 1,000 cases of beer just before Christmas and 700 for the New Year.

"A newcomer to the village is Mr Keith Crowther, chief barman at the Victoria Falls Hotel, who has now moved into a house 'on the other side of the line'... Both Christmas and New Year kept the Hotel staff busy. The Hotel was booked to capacity and all the festivities that had been laid on were very well patronised. The Old Year's Night dance, in particular, was a big success. Seven-year-old Patricia Scott (daughter of Mr Michael Scott, the assistant manager) made a delightful Fairy Princess who brought in 1966. Patricia is well practised in this important function as this is the third year running she has ably performed this task. Old Father Time was Andre de Wit, an apprentice cook, in heavy disguise. He was pushed from the crowded dance floor by two energetic clowns, five-year old Garry Scott and six-year old Michael Dodds, the latter the son of Mr Brian Dodds, the head waiter...

"The remodelling of the swimming pool has now been completed and it looks more inviting that ever, surrounded by small tables under gay umbrellas. The kiosk at the pool has also been opened for the sale of teas and cold drinks." (Rhodesia Railways Magazine, February 1966)

Victoria Falls Casino

The Victoria Falls Casino, later relaunched as the Makasa Sun Hotel, was opened in 1966 on the site immediately next to the Victoria Falls Hotel (and subsequently redeveloped in 1998/9 as The Kingdom). Preserved in the grounds was a section of the original trolley line down to the Falls. The casino was the first in the country and an added attraction advertised even by the Falls Hotel:

"After thrilling to the magnificence of the Victoria Falls, relax in sophisticated luxury at The Victoria Falls Hotel. Known to travellers of the world, the Hotel offers luxurious comfort and ideal facilities for viewing the magnificent Victoria Falls. In the evening you could visit the Victoria Falls Casino to experience the thrills of roulette, chemin-de-fer and baccarat." (Victoria Falls Hotel, 1960s)

The Victoria Falls Casino

The Casino was extended in 1969 with the addition of a new wing comprising 54 bedrooms and three luxury suites, at a cost of £175,000, the Hotel boasting four luxury suites and 102 bedrooms all with private bathroom, shower, radio and telephone.

More competition for the Hotel arrived on the northern bank of the river in 1968 with the development of the Mosi-oa-Tunya Intercontinental Hotel, located close to the Falls on the northern bank in Zambia. Fortunately plans for a ten-storey 'millionaire's playground,' with rooftop gardens overlooking the Falls, came to nothing (Roberts, 2021b).

Victoria Falls Airport

The Victoria Falls Airport was officially opened in 1967, allowing the growing town to service its own aviation arrivals and departures and avoiding the extra rigmarole of Zambian customs and immigration formalities.

"The staff of the Victoria Falls Hotel had an exceptionally busy Easter but cannot look forward to any respite for more than six months as the Hotel is booked to capacity right up to the end of October. The Rev Albert Jenkins, of the Railway Mission staff stationed in Livingstone, had a busy Easter at the Victoria Falls Hotel. On Good Friday he took services in the chapel; on Easter Saturday he conducted a marriage service, and on Easter Sunday he held three services and carried out a christening." (Rhodesia Railways Magazine, May 1967)

Visitors to the Hotel reached 21,975 in the operational year ending June 1967, and July was the busiest single month recorded to date with a total of 3,095 visitors, over half of which came from South Africa. The record numbers were largely due to the growth of regional air travel, with Air Rhodesia's successful 'Flame Lily' holiday packages linking Kariba and Hwange with the Falls. Groups of passengers from cruise liners arriving at the Cape now flew up to the Falls in a matter of hours.

"It is with great pleasure and pride that I record that the Victoria Falls Hotel known to travellers of the world, accommodated 21,975 visitors from 32 countries during the financial year ended June 30th 1967. This is an all-time record for the Hotel and I extend my warmest congratulations to the management and staff on this achievement." (Rhodesia Railways Magazine, October 1967)

Refreshing the Formula

African Spectacular

In keeping with changing world-wide hotel catering trends the all-inclusive tariff was phased out and replaced from 1st April 1968 with a bed-and-breakfast rate and an à la carte menu for the Dining Room. Together with the new service at the swimming pool, offering light luncheons at snack-bar prices, this fresh approach had a positive effect on trading and the financial losses of the previous years was reduced to only a small deficit in 1967, and to a record profit of some £32,945 in 1968.

A new traditional dance entertainment feature, the African Spectacular, was developed and performed nightly in a replica African village setting built behind the swimming pool.

Traditional Dancers

The show, which featured traditional dancers and cultural costumes from the local Falls region, soon became a popular and established part of a visit to the Falls. The talking point of the show was one of the performers lifting a section of steel railway line by his teeth. British comedian and actor Peter Sellers, who visited in the 1970s, described it enthusiastically as *"the best thing I have seen in Africa"* - a quote the Hotel would proudly use in its publicity advertising.

The reconstruction of the main Bulawayo to Victoria Falls strip road as a fully-tarred highway began in 1963 and the official opening was celebrated in 1968 with a vintage car rally from Bulawayo to the Falls, with over 40 competitors, many of who stayed at the Hotel to recuperate.

Jacket Still Required

The Hotel now had a total of 126 bedrooms, all boasting internal telephones, but only 72 with private bathrooms. The South African travel writer Lawrence G Green visited the Hotel in the late sixties on a road journey through Southern Rhodesia:

> *"I could not secure a private bathroom though I must say that the long Edwardian bath near my room could be filled with boiling water in a trice. The lavatory was always hard to flush and the distant thunder of the waterfall mocked my efforts. I had a mosquito net with holes in it but the fan ran perfectly all night."*

Road rally winner

Green was not enamoured by the relaxed clientele of the Hotel, whose dress style he felt was at odds with the Hotel's grand setting:

"Shorts do not go with chandeliers; bush shirts form a strange contrast with soft rugs and polished furniture. The final shock comes when you read this notice in the lounge: 'Gentlemen are requested to wear jackets and ties in the evening.' No doubt it is a necessary reminder though I have never encountered such a warning at a five star hotel.

"Yet I like the Victoria Falls Hotel... I like the corps of white-clad waiters with their pill-box caps, the sashed wine stewards who bring the right bottle in good time... But I wish the manager would take the centrepiece of artificial flowers away; after all, the hotel has its own farm, so bring on the flame lilies and orchids, wisteria and gardenias...

"I peered into the kitchen wing and saw that the kitchen was even larger than the dining-room. Here an impressive army of European chefs in tall white hats and African cooks bent over row after row of stoves. Here, deep in tropical Africa, is a temple of gastronomy that would have made Escoffier open his eyes. I could see every man going about his duties without hesitation. Cooking on this scale is organisation. Here it is, every department from soup to sweets, busy with its blending and heating amid billows of steam under the direction of

Tea with a view

the master mind, the chef de cuisine. Over the years this huge wing of the Hotel has transformed mountains of fresh-scrubbed vegetables, oceans of fish, all the delicacies of the civilised world. To this far corner of Africa have come oysters and caviar for royalty, turtle soup, Scotch salmon by the ton...

"They give you a map when you sign the register at this Hotel, for the place is so vast that you might lose your way...

"From the terrace you can watch trains crossing the Victoria Falls Bridge, the lights in the coach windows at night making a miniature railway spectacle that lingers on the screen of memory." (Green, 1968)

Anyone for tennis?

A New Lease of Life

On 1st February 1970 operation of the Hotel was leased by the Rhodesia Railways to external management, marking the end of over fifty years of direct management by the Railway Company. Mr Webster initially remained as Manager.

The lease was signed on the 4th February, by the Commissioner for Rhodesia Railways, Col. A Leslie, and the Chairman of the Rhodesian Breweries (Rhobrew), Mr J V Samuels. A suitable partner for the Hotel, Rhobrew claimed pioneer credentials older even than the Hotel's, tracing its origins back to 1898. In 1978 the name was changed to the Delta Corporation. Commenting on the agreement, Col. Leslie recorded:

> *"Rhodesia Railways have agreed to finance further improvements to the Hotel to bring it up to at least three-star standard and, together with the benefits that will flow from being part of a national chain of first class hotels, The Victoria Falls Hotel will be able to play an ever-increasing role of importance in Rhodesia's tourism development in the 'jumbo jet seventies'."* (Rhodesia Railways Magazine, March 1970)

Through its new managers, Rhodesian Breweries (Rhobrew), the Hotel was operated under the umbrella of the Southern Sun Hotel Corporation of Rhodesia Limited (known as Southern Sun), and part of a portfolio of hotels across the

Service at the Swimming Pool

The Hotel Lounge

country - including its neighbour the Makasa Sun - and resulting in significant operational benefits and commercial opportunities, especially in the South African market.

The Railway Company invested in an extensive $580,000 modernisation programme to bring the Hotel facilities and services up to standard. All the bedrooms were redecorated, air-conditioning fitted and a private bathroom provided for every room through the conversion of smaller rooms. A major phase of the works was the conversion of the old Summer Parlour above the Lounge into guest bedrooms. The public areas were also redecorated and recarpeted, the Pullman Room modernised and the Cocktail Bar fashionably re-styled as the modern 'I Presume Bar.' Following the successful completion of these developments the Hotel was upgraded to a three star rating.

Behind the Scenes

Mr Christopher Jarrett joined the Hotel's Accountants department in 1970 and was the Assistant Manager under Mr Webster when the modernisation works were undertaken. *"A guest,"* he recalls Mr Webster would often say, *"will forgive you anything as long as they have a comfortable bed and good food."*

He recalls the works, which were undertaken during the rainy season, encountered problems when water collected on the roof above the Lounge, threatening to collapse the ceiling. Holes had to be punched in the roof to drain the water, and staff positioned with large drums underneath to collect the cascades of water as they poured through the roof. The problems continued when water found its way into the Dining Room, dripping from the spinning ceiling fans!

Mr Jarrett had a keen interest in water lilies, collecting and growing many specimens in the Courtyard ponds, at one time counting nearly 150 blooms in just one pond. The flowers, which emerge overnight, would enchant guests who discovered them in the early mornings and be the topic of much conversation over breakfast. One species had leaves up to a metre wide. Today only the purple flowered 'Panama Pacific' variety still survives in the ponds.

Whilst giving great pleasure to many guests, the ponds were a source of annoyance to others, kept up at night by the loud calls of the frogs and toads which claim this little corner of paradise as their own. American guests in particular were not familiar or used to their calls, and the grounds contractor employed an enthusiastic African with a torch and a spear in an attempt to manage the problem. The result was a lesson in territorial behaviour in frogs, as no sooner had one singing male been removed another appeared, with no overall affect on the volume of their musical overtures.

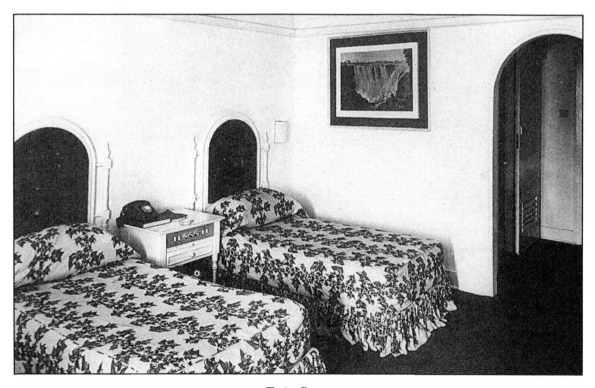

Twin Room

The ponds also occasionally caught the attention of local patrons of the Hotel bar leaving after an evening's entertainment, some of whom ended up taking a late night swim with the fish after one or two too many drinks. Intentionally or not, they would have at least kept the frogs quiet for a short while.

Mr Jarrett also recalls the antics of Mr Gregory, the groundsman, in change of baboon (and frog) control. The baboons soon learnt to recognise Mr Gregory in his attempts to stalk and shoot troublesome individuals, and he resorted to various disguises to buy their trust. He must have had more than the occasional confused glance from guests as he lurked around the grounds in a long overcoat and hat. The baboons however, knew full well his identity and intentions (Jarrett, 2015).

Leaving a Bad Taste

Australian cricket captain Ian Chappell recently recalled an incident which occurred during an unofficial invitational tour. On a rest day visit to the Falls, Chappell and a few other players relaxed over a couple of drinks at the bar at the Hotel.

"In 1972 I played in a double-wicket contest in [what is now] *Zimbabwe. On a rest day a few players were drinking in the back bar at the Victoria Falls Hotel.*

The I Presume Bar

We had been there a while when the proprietor suddenly told Basil D'Oliveira, a South African-born Cape Coloured man who played for England, that he had to leave the bar. I asked why. 'Because he's been swearing in front of my wife,' came the unconvincing reply.

"'Turn it up, mate,' I responded. 'There's a few of us been swearing, why pick on Basil?' The man insisted that Basil was the only one swearing, so we all put our unfinished beers on the bar and walked out." (Chappell, 2020)

The Man Who Built Victoria Falls

The early seventies saw an intense of development on the south bank, with the construction of new tourism facilities and supporting infrastructure, including housing suburbs, commercial centres, industrial premises, office and staff accommodation blocks and a diversification of new hotels.

Local construction company Gardini & Sons, under the skilled guidance of Carlo Gardini, were responsible for a large percentage of the construction projects, with Carlo becoming known as 'the man who built Victoria Falls.'

"Though that grand old lady of hostelries, the Victoria Falls Hotel, has been around considerably longer than Carlo ... he knows the old lady well. He has built a second storey here, added on 60 rooms there, done a major refurbishment another time. They understand each other. The Victoria Falls Casino Hotel, renamed the Makasa, the Sprayview (owned by the Gardini family), the A'Zambezi, the Rainbow, the Elephant Hills (the first small pretty version, with so much character) the Elephant Hills again (the present one that looks like Alcatraz); he built them all, with the houses, banks and shopping centres in between." (Meadows, 2000)

The fully air-conditioned, 40-room Peter's Motel opened in 1969 (later renamed the Victoria Falls Motel and later still the Sprayview Hotel), built, owned and operated by the Gardini family. The riverside A'Zambezi River Lodge, with 65 double and 15 family rooms, opened in 1972, and the centrally located 44-room Rainbow Hotel in 1974.

Elephant Hills Country Club

The Elephant Hills Country Club was opened in 1974, located a short distance upstream of the Falls on the high ridge Percy Clark had named Dale's Kopje. The four-star development included 20 rooms all with bath, phone, radio and air-conditioning. Facilities included squash courts, tennis courts, two swimming pools, bowling green, conference room, casino. and 18-hole international standard golf course designed by South African golfer Gary Player and opened in 1975. The course became known among golfers as 'more like a wildlife reserve than a golf course,' famed for its wildlife hazards - including interruptions by elephant, hippopotami and ball-stealing baboons - and giving rise to some rather curious local rule variations.

Southern Hospitality

Mr Peter Costeloe succeeded Mr Webster as Manager of the Hotel at the beginning of 1973, coming with experience from Raffles in Singapore, and marking the beginning of another period of significant change behind the scenes at the Hotel. Bookings, administration and marketing all becoming centralised through Southern Sun's head office in Salisbury.

At the time the country was in a state of economic isolation imposed by Britain and the United Nations following the announcement of U.D.I. in November 1965. These sanctions had largely failed by the early 1970s and even efforts to discourage tourists were unsuccessful in the main. Famous visitors during the 1970s included Peter Sellers, fellow British comedian Harry Secombe, the actresses Deborah

Outdoor chess on the lawns

Kerr and Ursula Andress, and pioneering South African heart transplant surgeon Christian Barnard.

"The Victoria Falls Hotel offers real Southern hospitality. Cosmopolitan, exotic, yet with a majestic sombre beauty, it offers so much... a bank, shop, hair salon and chapel. Air conditioned rooms and stately home style suites with private bathrooms and telephones. And what better place to hold a meeting than the conference room - with full facilities. At the Victoria Falls Hotel even a business meeting can become a vacation." (Victoria Falls Hotel, 1970s)

Over the decade the Hotel facilities were developed and now offered a range of indoor and outdoor sports, boasting a putting green, snooker, tennis, table tennis, outdoor chess, bowls and squash, as well as play facilities for children.

"Situated within easy access of the Victoria Falls the 'Greatest River Wonder in the World' - Victoria Falls Hotel offers the visitor a high standard of comfort, cuisine, and civility." (Victoria Falls Hotel, 1975)

Seventies Struggles

Following the Unilateral Declaration of Independence in 1965 life in the white-ruled, but internationally unrecognised, Republic of Rhodesia carried on much as normal, despite international sanctions, but the call for black majority rule was gaining momentum. The early 1970s saw an escalation in the struggle, with independence fighters launching strategic attacks across the Zambezi against communication and infrastructure facilities. Land mine incidents and train derailments followed over the subsequent months as the conflict escalated.

Ian Smith at the Falls

Eventually, on 9th January 1973, Smith announced the closure of border posts with Zambia, including Victoria Falls, until he received satisfactory assurances from the Zambian Government that it would no longer permit terrorists to operate and launch attacks against Rhodesia from within its territory. In response Zambia closed its border with Rhodesia on 1st February 1973 and the border area remained tense, with the Falls Bridge guarded and watched by troops on both sides.

In May 1973 a tragic incident occurred resulting in two Canadian tourists being killed by rifle fire from the Zambian side of the river whilst exploring the gorges below the Victoria Falls Hotel. The independence war gained intensity in the second half of the decade and tourism collapsed.

Bridge Over Troubled Water

On 25th August 1975 the Bridge was the site of unsuccessful peace talks, known as the 1975 Constitutional Conference. The talks, lasting nine and a half hours, took place aboard a South African Railways coach from the 'White Train,' used in the 1947 Royal Tour, positioned across the middle of the Bridge.

Supervised by South African Prime Minister John Vorster, the tense negotiations included Rhodesian Prime Minister Ian Smith, Zambian President Kenneth Kaunda, and representatives of the African National Council, led by Bishop Abel Muzorewa. The Rhodesian delegation sat on their side of the coach whilst nationalist representatives sat on the Zambian side. One account records the staff were apparently rather too liberal with the bar service and two members became intoxicated and disruptive, helping talks to continue throughout the day.

The Hotel hosted the South African and Rhodesian delegates. The talks failed and the troubles continued. In an effort to disrupt the rail service the lines were mined, and in December 1976 a passenger train was derailed south of Victoria Falls, an event which caused a cessation of the service until after the war.

Train talks on the bridge, with the Rhodesian flag flying

Motel Attacked

Insurgents directly targeted tourism in the town the evening of Saturday 30th October 1976 with an armed attack on the Peter's Motel in which one person died.

"African guerillas armed with grenades and automatic weapons attacked a motel at Victoria Falls late last night, killing one person and wounding two others, a spokesman for the Peters Motel said today... Between 20 and 30 guests were staying at the motel at the time of the raid, the spokesman said. Victoria Falls, just across the border from Zambia, is a favourite holiday resort for Rhodesians, many of whom flocked there this weekend for a golf tournament. Rhodesian security forces have organised a search for the commandos." (The Canberra Times, November 1976)

Elephant Hills Burns

Elephant Hills burns

The original Elephant Hills was destroyed by a fire caused by a SAM 7 heat-seeking missile launched from Zambia on 2nd November 1977. Apparently fired at a Rhodesia United Air Carriers light tourist aircraft which was circulating above the Falls, it missed its target and by chance landed on the thatched roof of the Hotel. The explosion was reportedly heard as far away as the Falls Airport. Luckily there were no casualties, but the hotel was completely gutted by the fire. The passengers from the light aircraft, piloted by Eddie Marucchi, apparently took it all in their stride. One, Mr Lief Bjorseth, was recorded as saying: *"It's not every day you get shot at - I got something extra for my money"* (Teede and Teede, 1994).

The hotel was destroyed, and remained a burnt-out ruin for the next several years, with only the golf course, a squash court and bar still operating.

Hotel Hit

By 1977 hotels and campsites were closing in the face of security concerns, including the Rainbow Hotel, mothballed until more favourable tourism conditions returned. Upstream of the Falls the Zambezi Camp was closed and access to the town controlled as a cordon of security surrounded the tourism resort.

On 19th December 1977 several people were wounded when the town and Hotel came under mortar attack from the northern bank.

"Eight civilians were wounded when the Victoria Falls resort was shelled from neighbouring Zambia, the military command reported yesterday, according to Associated Press... In the 25-minute shelling a popular tourist hotel, the Victoria Falls, was damaged. A military communiqué later said one person was seriously hurt. The rest suffered minor injuries. The command did not say whether the injured were Rhodesians or foreign tourists. Rhodesian troops based at the falls fired back across the Zambezi River dividing the two countries. 'The attacking positions were silenced,' the communiqué said. Several mortar shells exploded in the town of 4,500 people as foreign and local tourists were dining or gambling at the casino, residents said." (The Canberra Times, December 1977a)

Local resident, Juliet Bell, was at the Hotel that night and recalled the incident:

"I was there with a party of friends in the early evening when the first mortar came in about the swimming pool. A few people moved out of the area but not many - the River Boys were playing and everyone enjoyed those evenings so much and explosions were often heard in the distance, so no one bothered too much. There were not many tourists but the gardens were still busy, mainly army and police reserves and locals. Then another mortar landed much closer and we all left the garden in a hurry for the lounges inside, lay on the floor - away from the plate glass windows and under cushions from the chairs - and stayed there for ages while the mortars were spraying the town as well. The armoured cars were called out in the end and once all was quiet we had free drinks in the bar till very late. I couldn't stop sneezing for hours after! Nervous reaction! People were asking me if I took cover in the fish pond!" (Bell, 2020)

A week later, on Christmas Eve, the town came under attack again, although without casualties.

"Rhodesian troops near the tourist resort of Victoria Falls came under fire from Zambia on Christmas Eve in the second attack on the area in a week, military headquarters said yesterday. A Christmas Day communiqué said a security forces position near the town, packed with Christmas holidaymakers, was subjected to 'an unprovoked rocket and small arms attack' on Saturday night. No damage or casualties were caused, it stated." (The Canberra Times, December 1977b)

Emergency Procedures

With the ongoing independence struggle and closure of the border Victoria Falls was the scene of much military activity.

"There was no particular reason to suspect that there might be an attack on the Hotel as the Victoria Falls area was a hive of Security Force activity from the outset, although precautions were taken after the destruction of the Elephant Hills. Care had always to be taken not to alarm guests, nor to scare off would-be visitors, and after a failed mortar attack on the Victoria Falls area, with one off target shell narrowly missing the laundry outbuilding, causing slight damage, it was decided to warn guests by sticking notices onto their bathroom mirrors. The Hotel quickly found that the stickers were being removed by guests as souvenirs, and new stocks had to be constantly reprinted!" (Moore, 2012)

In the early 1970s tourist arrivals to the country hovered at around 340,000 per annum. By 1979 there were only 79,000 - the lowest total since 1963. Over sixty percent of the Hotel's guests came from South Africa, as international arrivals evaporated.

"Tourism was badly affected by the war and the country's hotels survived only because of support from Government in the form of subsidies and subsidised travel by local and international visitors. To help the battered tourism sector, the national airline and hotel groups introduced the Super Six scheme, in which guests went on air and road packages for up to six nights at significantly discounted prices. The scheme met with reasonable success and the number of visitors to hotels, including the Victoria Falls Hotel, was remarkable given the overall situation in the country." (Creewel, 2004)

The border with Zambia remained officially closed until January 1980.

EMERGENCY NOTICE

IN THE EVENT OF AN ATTACK ON THE HOTEL

Turn all lights out.

Stay away from windows.

Lie down on the floor close to an interior wall.

Wait for further instructions.

Sikes Bulawayo

Hotel emergency notice

Minefield Menace

Extensive anti-personnel minefields were laid along 220 kilometres of border between Victoria Falls and downstream to Mlibizi during the latter period of the war, with Victoria Falls town encircled in a protective 'cordon sanitaire.' Containing some of the highest densities of mines in the world, the minefields would continue to pose a serious threat to people and wildlife for decades after the war. It would take until 2015 before the vast majority of these minefields would be cleared (Victoria Falls Bits and Blogs, June 2015).

Independence forces were rumoured to be actively planning and preparing fighters in Zambia with the intent of launching a major invasion across the Zambezi. To prevent opposition forces crossing the Falls Bridge the road surface was removed and in late 1978 and the Bridge set with explosives, ready to blow a critical section should it be necessary (Burrett and Murray, 2013).

Road to Peace

After the failure of a nationally negotiated power-sharing agreement, negotiated with moderate independence groups in 1978 but unrecognised by the two main exiled liberation groups, the British government invited all parties to peace talks in London. After fourteen weeks of talks, and with Rhodesia and Zambia on the brink of full scale war, the Lancaster House Agreement was finally signed on 21st December 1979.

International economic sanctions were lifted in late 1979 and the country reverted to temporary British rule until elections could be held. Lord Soames was appointed by the British government as Governor-Designate, arriving in Salisbury on 12th December. On 21st December 1979 a cease-fire was finally announced. The Falls Bridge reopened to rail traffic and in the last week of December 1979 a team of workmen restored the road surface.

Opposite sides meet on the Bridge, December 1979

New Beginnings

The Zimbabwe flag proudly flies at the Hotel

National elections were held in February 1980, with the Zimbabwe African National Union-Patriotic Front, led by Robert Mugabe, receiving 63 percent of the vote. On 18th April 1980 interim British rule ended with divided Rhodesia becoming independent Zimbabwe.

In a wave of reconciliation, optimism and hope for the future, peace returned to the country, together with the tourists. The total number of visitors to Zimbabwe rebounded to 238,000 in 1980 - triple those of the previous year, with the vast majority, some 95 percent, arriving by air - and 314,000 in 1981. Tourists from South Africa made up only ten percent of the Hotel's guests, with the Hotel rebuilding its primary markets in the United States and United Kingdom.

Independence saw a new Manager for the Hotel, with Mr John C Creewel becoming General Manager in 1982. The Southern Sun Group re-branded as Zimbabwe Sun Hotels, with the Victoria Falls Hotel now part of a group of 12 hotels nationwide, the largest hotel group in the country, later becoming known as Zimsun Leisure Group.

The Hotel now had 138 rooms, including 15 suites, with all rooms equipped with radio, taped music and telephone, and each with its own private bathroom with shower. The Dining Room catered to a capacity of 180 diners.

A Hotel publicity brochure from the early 1980s describes the 'Patrician Bar,' promoted as a traditional cocktail bar, with a capacity of 50 to 60, and offering 'sophisticated elegance combined with an atmosphere of resort informality.' The smaller 'Plebs Bar,' was described as 'an informal meeting place for those who prefer a pub atmosphere,' and the 'Deep End Bar' by the pool offered 'long cooling cocktails.'

Continental breakfast was served on the terrace for those guests who preferred to greet the new day amidst the splendour of the surroundings. A marimba band entertained with traditional percussion instruments whilst guests enjoyed a buffet lunch, and a terrace barbecue - braai in the adopted Afrikaans slang - in the evening provided an entertaining social diversion for guests.

In 1982 another tragic incident hit the country's tourist trade when a group of six international tourists were kidnapped and eventually murdered by political dissidents. The group, comprising two Americans, two Australians and two British tourists, were travelling between Victoria Falls and Bulawayo. Tourism again slumped in the shadow of negative international headlines and travel warnings.

Kissinger's Crocodile Tale

Henry Kissinger, former US Secretary of State, visited the Falls in 1982, attending a luncheon whilst staying at the Hotel.

"The occasion was a special luncheon at which the Anglo-American Corporation entertained Henry Kissinger, the U.S. statesman, during his tour of Zimbabwe. It was held in a private room overlooking the spectacular Falls and the historic bridge which marks the boundary between Zimbabwe and Zambia... All six dishes on the menu were made from local ingredients and included a mousseline of smoked trout (as an optional starter), guineafowl and beef Wellington. But the star turn was the crocodile cocktail, which must receive my accolade as the most novel dish of the year." (Caterer & Hotelkeeper Magazine, 1982)

Time to spare

Visit of Princess Anne

Her Royal Highness Princess Anne stayed at the Hotel in 1982 as part of a tour of six African countries in her capacity as President of the Save the Children Fund. The Princess stayed in the Queen's Suite, which had hosted her grand-parents in 1947 and now renamed the Livingstone Suite, for two nights at the end of October 1982. Whilst at the Falls the Princess undertook a tour of the Rainforest and a river cruise - brief breaks in a busy schedule which also included visiting the Jairos Jiri centre for severely handicapped children. Mr Creewel recorded his thanks to staff in a memorandum soon after the visit, the Royal party having been 'most comfortable' and 'very impressed with the friendliness of good service they had received.'

Eightieth Anniversary Year

Mr Mark Charles Jones became General Manager of the Hotel in March 1984, after a period as the Resident Manager at the Monomatapa Hotel in Harare, part of the Zimsun group. Mr Creewel moved in the opposite direction, becoming the General Manager at the Monomatapa.

In celebration of the Hotel's eightieth anniversary year, a series of upgrades and events were planned, aimed at achieving the four-star rating and spurred on by friendly rivalry with the neighbouring Makasa Sun. In a break with tradition, the Hotel exterior was painted a delicate mint green, and the interiors refreshed in a matching green and white theme, with the Dining Room in 'elegant pink and white.' The recognition was duly awarded and credited to the untiring efforts of Mr Jones and his staff to improve the standard of service and cuisine at the Hotel.

*A four-star team. Mr Jones and the staff of the Hotel
ready for the Eightieth Anniversary Celebrations*

The main anniversary celebrations were held over the weekend of 7-9th December 1984, with a special programme of events, including champagne breakfasts in the Bridge Room (adjoining the Lounge), lunch on the banks of the Zambezi, cocktails and canapés on the Terrace and lawns and a formal Birthday Banquet in the Pullman Suite.

Dr Frederick Shava, Minister of Labour, Manpower Planning and Social Welfare, was guest of honour reflecting the Hotel's status as the principal employer in the region.

"One highlight of the occasion was the presentation of long service awards by the Minister of Labour, Manpower Planning and Social Service, Dr Shava, to Mr Mate Masuku, the longest serving member on the hotel staff, who has been with the hotel for 33 years, and Mr Patrick Guri, at 64 the oldest serving member of staff who has 32 years service." (Hotel & Catering Magazine, 1984)

Mr Jones cuts the cake

Eightieth Anniversary service in the garden

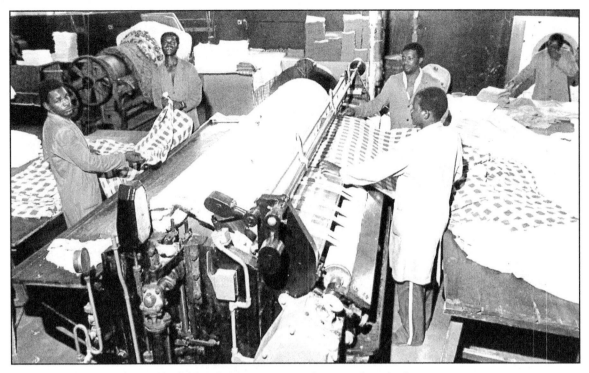

Behind the scenes in the Hotel Laundry

The coal-fired boilers

Mr Jones with the support of Mr Mike Routledge, Managing Director, and Mr Perrie Hennessy, Operations Director, was responsible for a complement of 240 staff servicing the Hotel's 132 bedrooms and seven suites.

Behind the scenes ran an efficient industrial scale operation in catering, laundry and other support services, not to mention building and plant equipment management and maintenance.

The Marimba Band in action

The grounds offered guests an extension of the Hotel's services, with afternoon tea on the lawns, entertained by a traditional marimba band, and bar and food service at the swimming pool.

Poolside

The dining menu now proudly included Zimbabwe's finest Inyanga trout, warthog steak and impala venison, to be washed down with local Zimbabwean wines. Mr Jones recorded:

"We import very little. There are small allocations made of smoked salmon, and prawns from Tanzania, plus a few wines from South Africa. But, as this country produces some of the finest beef, lamb and pork in the world, our emphasis is on meat rather than seafood... We have to remember that the closest large town is 450 km away... There was one occasion when a conference party came with their own printed menus, which included avocados. The latter didn't arrive on the truck, so we had to improvise with paw paw, which we hastily assured the delegates was the local version of the avocado pear." (Caterer & Hotelkeeper Magazine, 1984)

Mr Jones recalls that a notable visitor to the Hotel during his tenure was Sir Geoffrey Howe, the British Secretary of State for Foreign and Commonwealth Affairs, on a literally flying visit to the Falls. Delayed, his private flight was supposed to wait for him, but ended up taking off without him. Stranded at the Hotel, it took all Mr Jones' powers of persuasion, together with the help of the local Air Zimbabwe office, to get Johannesburg Air Traffic Control to turn the plane back to collect him.

The Dining Room decked out for Christmas 1984

Mr Jones left the Hotel after a successful anniversary year, departing in April 1985. A farewell dinner held in his honour included a special Hotel-themed menu, including a desert entitled 'Mint Green and Mangoes, a parting view from the Courtyard' (Jones, 2015).

A memorable member of staff during this period, known to many guests, was Mr Ordwell Makamure, the Hotel concierge. He is remembered by many for his jacket - heavily emblazoned with a variety of pins and badges from all over the world, and a tradition followed by successive Concierges at the Hotel.

'Welcome to the Victoria Falls Hotel'

Africa's Adrenalin Capital

During the late 1980s and early 1990s Victoria Falls saw the development of thrill-seeking adventure activities, earning the town a new reputation as the 'adrenalin capital of Africa.' In addition to the traditional tourism activities of game drives and river safaris, new 'high-intensity' activities, such as white-water rafting and bungee jumping attracted a younger generation of travellers to the Falls.

New Managers

> *"In the late 80s and early 90s among the managers of the Hotel were Terry Ryan, as well as New Zealander Ken Lyall, who was a stickler for high standards among his management team and was never to be seen without his suit, even in the extreme heat of a mid-summer's day."* (Creewel, 2004)

Stone Dynamics

The Stone Dynamics Gallery opened at the Hotel in 1986, showcasing the best of Zimbabwe's artists and their finest works. Zimbabwe has a strong tradition of stone carving and sculpture, recognised for its unique style and quality by artists and collectors around the world.

On Location

Richard Chamberlain and Sharon Stone stayed at the Hotel during filming 'King Solomon's Mines' (released 1985) and its sequel, 'Allan Quatermain and the Lost City of Gold' (1986). British travel journalist, actor and comedian Michael Palin visited the Victoria Falls in 1991, breaking a rib whilst white-water rafting during recording of his B.B.C. television series and epic journey from 'Pole to Pole.' Recuperating at the Hotel he recorded:

"The whole place feels like a very well appointed Old Folk's home. The price for this soft-furnished cosseting is re-entry into the world of regulations. The 'I Presume' Bar has a sign warning that between 7.00 and 11.30, dress is 'Smart Casual. No Denims, No T-Shirts, No Takkies.'" (Palin, 1992)

The Hotel was also the feature location for a Sherlock Holmes television film, starring Christopher Lee (later Sir) and Patrick McNee, in 'The Incident at Victoria Falls,' released in 1992. The film portrays Holmes and Watson in older age, asked to undertake one last case before retirement and includes many shots of the Hotel.

Ninety Glorious Years

Mr Mark Sonenscher arrived as General Manager of the Hotel in 1993, overseeing the Hotel's 90th anniversary celebrations in the following year. On 11th June 1994 an Edwardian themed celebratory cocktail party was held on the front lawns, and the main anniversary event was held in November, including a garden party, banquet and ball, musicians and entertainment, all with a historical period theme.

The focal point of the anniversary celebrations was the reopening of the Dining Room, which had been extensively refurbished and was re-launched as the Livingstone Room. In a taste of things to come the redevelopment recaptured the historic feel of the Hotel, enhanced to the finest standards. The room was ornately refurnished with opulent gold decorated walls and elegant period furniture and fittings. Air-conditioning was installed, whilst still retaining period features such as the old-fashioned ceiling fans and high oval windows. The strict Hotel dress code was still actively enforced, but often diplomatically handled by Restaurants Manager Mr Phillip James, who had access to a small store of spare jackets and a selection of ties for those caught unprepared.

Crown Prince Albert of Monaco also stayed at the Hotel during the year and a host of celebrities, including Cliff Richard (later Sir), Oprah Winfrey, Jenny Agutter and Jack Lemmon, visited during the period.

The Hotel Reborn

In the early 1990s it was recognised that the Hotel was in need of substantial renovation, and plans were drawn up for a significant refurbishment of the buildings.

The project was co-ordinated for Zimbabwe Sun Hotels by their development manager, Mr Graham Johnson. Mr Graham Viney acted as historical, architectural and interior design consultant, Mr Mike Clinton of Clinton & Evans as architect, and Gardini and Sons as builders, with Mr Carlo Gardini continuing a long association with the Hotel.

The original plans envisaged a grand Victorian feel to the Hotel, with glass enclosed conservatories, ornate ironwork and marble flooring, before under the guidance of Mr Viney it was decided to recapture and restore the Hotel's original period character and style. The plans were redrawn with a focus on the enhancing of original period features such as the columned porches and stepped verandas, and restoration of the main axis through the middle of the Hotel buildings.

The main driveway

Mr Viney recalls:

"The veranda had disappeared and was enclosed with aluminium sliders and glass louvers; there was a horrible breeze-block erection containing a braai area just below it. Crazy paving reigned supreme. Of course each age has its look, but here everything possible seemed to have been done to iron out the Hotel's original architecture and character. The Lounge had bright green fitted industrial carpeting, wagon-wheel furniture (once a grim brown now painted a hospital white) and there were endless pyramids of chrysanthemums in plastic containers. The aircon - pitched at freezing - contended with the smell of braai-grilled meat.

"There was nowhere to sit outside and enjoy that marvellous view. That view which was in fact a grandly conceived imperial architectural axis, starting at the station, down through the Hotel's entrance, across its courtyard, through the main Lounge, out onto the veranda and finally centred far beyond on the graceful steel bridge spanning the great gorge, with the spray of the Falls rising behind it. Unbelievably, it had become largely obscured - my very first thought was that this must at all costs be reinstated and this is again one of the great joys of the place for guests today.

"The Hotel's architecture is often described as 'Edwardian,' but this is, of course, not strictly true for a hotel built during the First World War. It is not even Neo-Georgian, really. Indeed, the original architecture is a stylish, and for its day curiously original and modern, East African Coast colonial hybrid, presaging elements of the art deco taste which appeared internationally in the following two decades. It had real merit and where possible, with the aid of the original plans found in the Bulawayo Railway Museum and photographs in the Harare Archives, it was restored. The interiors, though by no means a museum recreation, are conceived to be redolent of the inter-war colonial era and the great age of glamorous travel." (Viney, 2015)

On 15th January 1996, for the only time in its long history, the Hotel was temporarily closed to visitors. Five hundred workers swarmed over the site as during ten weeks of closure the Hotel was extensively stripped, gutted and rebuilt. The old coal fired boilers were removed and replaced with electric hot-water geysers, and the hot and cold water pipes replaced throughout the buildings. The steam operated laundry was finally replaced and upgraded, and a new electricity sub-station was built. The entire building was also fitted with modern smoke detectors, fire alarms and water sprinkler systems.

The restored frontage of the Hotel

The front extensions and sliding glass windows which had enclosed the veranda and face of the Hotel were removed and the original columned facade of the building restored. The old bar was refurbished and renamed as Stanley's Room, with hand painted murals showing the old viewing towers. On the opposite side of the Lounge the old luncheon/buffet room was converted into the luxurious Bulawayo Room, a quiet and comfortable rest and reading room, under the imposing gaze of the Matabele King, Lobengula, whose portrait dominates the room. The Lounge itself was furnished to luxurious standards. The second-floor bedrooms were upgraded into luxury suites, with spectacular views over the Hotel lawns to the gorges and Bridge. One feature of the fifties improvements preserved by the redevelopment were the twin spiral staircases, much to Mr Gardini's pleasure, as he regarded them with much pride.

The Hotel interiors were extensively redecorated and refurbished in a classic period style, but with a full range of modern conveniences and amenities that included upgraded air-conditioning and satellite television in all bedrooms. Carpets were ordered from Egypt, curtains from London, Lloyd Loom styled chairs from Bali, and four-poster beds from Cape Town. The Reception Hall was also restored to a period style with wood panelled counters. The Hotel's Manager, Mr Sonenscher, reported: *"The aim was to recapture the Edwardian elegance of the hotel and bring it up to the highest international standards in every aspect of its operation"* (Creewel, 2004).

The corridors were repainted in dark Pompeii Red and covered with archive photographs and memorabilia celebrating the rich history of the Hotel - old black and white images of the early Falls settlement and original Hotel buildings; vintage cruise liner, railway and aviation tourism posters advertising southern Africa and the wonder of the Falls to the world; and souvenirs of royal visits.

The renovations cost some $6.5 million. At the end of this huge undertaking the Hotel was re-launched as The Victoria Falls Hotel, and widely recognised as having regained its status as one of the world's most iconic hotels. For its logo the Hotel readopted a version of the Hotel's original first logo, featuring the lion and sphinx, re-created from a broken piece of crockery found in a old rubbish pit in the grounds.

Poetic Licence

A main feature of the redesigned Lounge were two large oil paintings, commissioned for the Hotel and showing His Majesty King George V, based on a painting by Sir Arthur S Cope, and Her Majesty Queen Mary, from a painting by Sir S H William Llewellyn.

> *"The Hotel's manager fretted most about the huge oils Mr Viney had ordered... They showed George V on the deck of a dreadnought as First Sea Lord, and Queen Mary in her tiara... Surely, the man said, they would offend ordinary Zimbabweans, who suffered for decades at English hands. He needn't have worried. On the day the portraits were hung, Mr Viney found a crowd of 40 workers staring at them. An old man was shaking his head. 'That is wrong,'*

The Main Lounge

View of the rising spray of the Falls from the Hotel lawns

the man said, pointing. 'The pictures?' No, he replied, it was the stuffed buffalo head between them. 'For a king, a buffalo is disrespectful. It must be a lion.'" (McNeil, 1997)

Lawns and Terraces

As part of the redevelopment of the grounds, the concrete barbecue area, which had been developed from the outdoor chess board on the front lawns, was demolished and restored to garden. The flagstone path to the lower terrace and gorge viewpoint, complete with flag-pole, was developed, redeveloping and expanding on a focal feature of the early Hotel.

The view from the veranda was re-established through selective pruning back of the invasive bush and tree growth, leaving feature specimens of indigenous trees, such as the magnificent Msasa (*Brachystigea spiciformis*) on the lawns below the terrace, which is thought to be over 200 years old. Its partner on the lawns, the large Mtshibi tree (*Guibourtia coleosperma*), unfortunately became diseased and had to be cut back, although it is now regaining its shape and symmetry.

Swimming Pool

The swimming pool was rejuvenated with the redevelopment of four adjoining

Swimming Pool pergola

pavilions and pergolas complete with open plan arches, extensive tiling and restoration of the pool fountain feature.

Fountain feature

The Jungle Junction

A new outdoor restaurant was established, named the Jungle Junction after the nickname for the flying boat stop-over point on the Zambezi above the Falls. The restaurant was developed on the site previously used for the Africa Spectacular show, for 30 years a scene of nightly entertainment. The show was relocated to the Elephant Hills Hotel, now redeveloped and also under the Zimbabwe Sun Hotels umbrella. A 'taster' show, however, still forms the nightly introduction to dining at the Jungle Junction.

The Jungle Junction

The horseshoe shaped thatched structure echoes the Hotel's period feel with classic columns and central ornamental pond and fountain following the design of those in the Courtyard.

During the redevelopments in the main building of the Hotel the mosaic compass, long hidden in the original veranda floor, was rediscovered. The mosaic was skilfully removed and relocated by Mr Gardini to become a focal point of the Jungle Junction (Creewel, 2004).

The Stone Dynamics Gallery relocated from their original location near the main lounge to an open-air setting in the grounds next to the restaurant.

View of the Jungle Junction

The mosaic compass

Stables Wing Extension

One of the most significant extensions to the Hotel in recent decades was the construction of the new Stables Wing, opened in 1997. The area was previously the site of the manager's house, which was relocated to a new building beyond the tennis courts and overlooking the gorge.

During the construction of the wing work had to be stopped when graves were discovered. The site turned out to be an old burial area, and local spiritual leaders were brought in to perform cleansing rituals before the remains were respectfully removed and reburied.

Centred around its own shaded courtyard gardens, four mature palm trees were planted as the focal feature. Sourced from Chiredzi, in the south-east of the country, their relocation was a major challenge. Also planted in the gardens were flowering shrubs from Brazil known as 'Yesterday, today and tomorrow' (*Brunfelsia pauciflora*), named after the scented flowers which bloom dark purple and turn to lilac and then white, over a period of three days.

The Stables Wing

The Stables Wing Courtyard

The wing included a viewing tower, replicating a feature of the original Hotel buildings, and from which the rising spray from the Falls could be seen (before the development of The Kingdom and subsequent tree growth shielded the view). Designed to accommodate demand from U.S. and other international tour groups the wing comprised 42 executive twin rooms as well as two honeymoon suites.

The bathrooms included large period style free standing iron baths with classic 'ball and claw' styled feet. All bathrooms across the Hotel were refurbished during late 1997 and 1998, returned to a classic Edwardian period style.

Pullman Suite Retired

In 1998 the Pullman Suite, site of many important and influential conferences and meetings over 48 years, was converted into an exclusive shop and gallery.

The Victoria Falls Partnership

A significant development for the Hotel in the late 1990s was the partnership established with another premier home-grown hospitality operation, Meikles Africa Ltd. The group has a long and proud history in the country, tracing its origins back to 1892, and includes in its portfolio the famous five-star Meikles Hotel in Harare, first opened in 1915. Meikles had been earlier linked with the Hotel during the 1970s when it had formed an operational and marketing alliance with the Southern Sun group.

Mr Roy Meiring, Meikles Africa chief executive, opened negotiations on a possible joint venture with Zimbabwe Sun chief executive Mr John Smith - leading to the formation of The Victoria Falls Partnership on 1st August 1998, with 50 percent equal ownership between Zimbabwe Sun and Meikles Africa.

Mr Karl Snater, a senior member of the Meikles Hotel management team, joined the Falls Hotel as Deputy General Manager in 1999 and focused on introducing Meikles management practices and quality standards. Other members of the Meikles team seconded to the Hotel included Mr David Seaman, who took up the post of Operations Manager in early 2002.

View from the Courtyard through original wing of the Hotel

Leading the Way

In 1999 the Hotel joined an exclusive and elite group of premier tourism resorts, the 'Leading Hotels of the World' consortium.

"The Hotel became a member of the Leading Hotels of the World in 1999 and achieved ISO 9002 quality standard status the same year... The Hotel also joined the Virtuoso network of leading hotels." (Creewel, 2004)

By the end of the 1990s an average of 300,000 tourists were visiting the Zimbabwe side of the Falls each year.

Front view of Hotel

Emerged Railway Properties

After the formation of the National Railways of Zimbabwe in 1980, the non-railway assets of Rhodesia Railways, which included the Victoria Falls Bridge and the Hotel, were transferred to the ownership of the Emerged Railways Properties (Private) Limited (E.R.P.). An interstate company, jointly owned by the Governments of Zambia and Zimbabwe, the E.R.P. was formally established in 1997.

Railway Revival

Towards the end of the 1990s there was a revival in travel by special train, with first-class luxury train services such as the South African Blue Train and Rovos Rail making frequent visits to the Victoria Falls with their passengers staying at the Hotel. Regional and international aviation arrivals also rose rapidly, peaking in the late 1990s.

"The years 1988 to 1999 were to become known as the boom years for Zimbabwean tourism. Large numbers of visitors arrived and demand for accommodation reached unprecedented levels, especially in Victoria Falls. New hotels and lodges were built, including Ilala Lodge, and air services to the local airport expanded to include up to three flights from Johannesburg each day, two flights from Harare, one from Bulawayo and various others from Botswana and Namibia. At one point a Harare-London service from Air Zimbabwe included a stop at Victoria Falls, making it a direct destination for international travellers from abroad for the first time." (Creewel, 2004)

The Grand Old Lady of the Falls

Into the New Millennium

The beginning of the new millennium was not an easy period for Zimbabwe or its tourism sector. National political and economic uncertainties resulted in social upheaval, negative international media coverage and economic collapse. Annual arrivals to Victoria Falls dropped from 190,000 in 1999 to average below 84,000 between 2002 and 2010.

In 2003 David Seaman became the Hotel's new General Manager, overseeing a period focussing on the Hotel's commitment to quality and first-class service, as well as centenary celebrations, but inheriting occupancy levels of only 22 percent.

The Victoria Falls Partnership invested in an exercise to improve the visitor facilities at the Falls with the upgrade and redevelopment of the car parking facility opposite the entrance to the Rainforest. The work included the surfacing of the parking area and creation of formal parking bays, pavements as well as the construction of market facilities for local independent artists and traders. The new facility was officially opened in December 2003.

A Grand Old Lady

In celebration of the Hotel's centenary, a major landmark for the Hotel, 2004 included a year-long calendar of anniversary events, special offers and promotions. A special weekend event was held in June, toasting one hundred years of service.

The celebratory year was launched on 11th December 2003, with a special reception at the Hotel for selected guests from the Victoria Falls community and key figures of the tourism industry. Speaking at the event the Hotel's new General Manager Mr Seaman said:

> "This is not simply the anniversary of the hotel alone. It is also the anniversary of the Victoria Falls community itself... The history of the Hotel is filled with people and events, pomp and pageantry, times of great challenges and times of woe, times of joy and excitement. Among the people serving on the staff have been colourful and talented characters, some of the finest hospitality people this country has known, serving at all levels within the different departments.

> "The Victoria Falls Hotel is rich in tradition and stands at a par with other famous names in hospitality, from Raffles in Singapore to the Mount Nelson in the Cape and from The Savoy in London to The Ritz in New York. It may be different in shape and size and scope to these... but it is identical... in holding

fast to the notion of splendid service at all times in an unstinting and unceasing fashion."

In proposing a toast to the next 100 years, he drew attention to the Hotel's adopted name, 'The Grand Old Lady of the Falls' and said the Hotel could look forward with confidence.

"The Victoria Falls Hotel has been described as more than simply a hotel; it is an institution rich in history and culture, with an impact on tourism commensurate with its position as the first international-standard hotel in the country and now one of the most luxurious and elegant in all Africa." (Creewel, 2004)

Mr Fungai Makani became General Manager of the Hotel in the second half of 2004, the Hotel's first black African manager and taking over the Hotel during a difficult period of low tourism arrivals. After many years of strict enforcement, Mr Makani relaxed the dress code restrictions in the Livingstone Room in a effort to attract more clients to the Hotel's prime dining facility.

Courtyard view with old trolley at far end

The Centenary Room

Centenary Room

To mark its centenary, the Hotel opened a new executive conference and private dining venue to host meetings, lunches and dinners for up to 18 people.

Situated adjacent to the Hotel's main Dining Room, the Centenary Room overlooks the central courtyard, with a small terrace area on which refreshments are served during breaks in meetings. The room has an interesting history, having over the years been a card room, an office and most recently a billiards room, housing a full-sized snooker table. (The table is now in the private ownership of Victoria Falls resident Mr Kevin van Jaarsveldt.)

The new venue was officially opened by the Minister of Environment and Tourism, Francis Nhema, at a special dinner hosted by The Victoria Falls Hotel Partnership. In his speech Mr Nhema paid tribute to the Hotel's proud history:

"The Victoria Falls Hotel this year marks its 100th anniversary and becomes the first Zimbabwean hotel to celebrate a centenary. This is no mean achievement and I would like to congratulate all the parties involved in this most welcome development, from the National Railways of Zimbabwe to Zimsun Leisure

Group and Meikles Africa Hotels, and from the management and staff of the hotel past and present to the hundreds of thousands of people who have stayed here during the past century of operations.

"Victoria Falls as a town owes its existence to this Hotel, for the coming of the Hotel in 1904 brought with it the establishment of a tourism infrastructure and a tourism sector. So when we talk about the centenary of the Hotel we are in fact talking about the centenary of this town and its tourism sector and, extending this further, perhaps it is indeed the real centenary of our national tourism sector as a whole.

"I understand this Hotel is known as the 'Grand Old Lady of the Victoria Falls' and, having had a good look around during the historical tour a few hours ago, I can see how much heritage and tradition we have within its buildings and grounds. What is all the more remarkable is how the old and the new have combined to bring to guests every modern convenience side by side with this history and all the traditions.

"This must truly be the most elegant hotel in Zimbabwe and one of the finest hotels on the entire African continent." (Victoria Falls Hotel, July 2004)

Entrance to the Hotel

Under an African Sun

Zimbabwe Sun Limited was re-branded as African Sun Limited in 2008, reflecting its pan-African holdings, including operations in Zimbabwe, South Africa, Nigeria and Ghana. Its portfolio of hotels in Zimbabwe included the Elephant Hills Resort and Conference Centre, and The Kingdom at Victoria Falls as well as the ongoing joint management of the Victoria Falls Hotel with Meikles Africa Ltd.

Challenging Conditions

Tourism slowly recovered from the lows of 2003, although difficult economic and operating conditions made challenging work for a succession of managers at the Hotel, including Mr Isaac Mpala (2006-7), Acting Manager Mr Lawrence Mattock (2008) and Mr Tamuka Macheka (2008).

The situation was so bad that even the fence at the foot of the front lawns was stolen in 2008. The friendly family of bushbuck which had been resident in the Hotel grounds for so many years found their freedom, to be replaced by the appearance of less charming visitors, with buffalo discovered one morning feeding on the lawns. With elephant and hippopotamus also attracted to the lush well-watered grounds, finding funds for a replacement fence was one of many important priorities.

Hotel occupancy sank to twenty-five percent at the height of the crisis in 2008 and menu prices had to be changed hourly to keep up with inflation. Staff salaries became virtually worthless and supplies and stocks almost impossible to source.

Turning the Tide

Mr Karl Snater became General Manager of the Hotel in February 2009, returning to guide the Hotel through difficult economic days, after a decade of spiralling hyper-inflation had resulted in the crippling of the economy and collapse of the Zimbabwe dollar. Also returning to the Hotel was his wife, Nicole, as Product Development Manager. The couple had met ten years earlier while Mr Snater had been Deputy General Manager of the Hotel.

Operating through some of the most difficult times in the Hotel's long history, Mr Snater concentrated on rebuilding the Hotel's high standards of quality and service. Michael Ovens was hired as Executive Chef, playing a significant role in delivering a five-star catering service and menu.

Guests arrive

The US dollar was subsequently adopted in 2009 as the main trading currency within a multi-currency market, marking the turning point in the economic crisis with stability returning to the trading markets and the slow recovery of tourism. The Zimbabwe dollar was finally officially decommissioned in 2015 at a rate of 35 quadrillion (Z$35,000,000,000,000,000) to one US dollar (Reserve Bank of Zimbabwe, 2015).

Mr Snater recalls the turning point came in June 2009 with a staff strike, resulting in the dismissal of a third of the workforce. Staff had suffered incredible hardships through the crisis, and morale was at rock bottom. However those that remained were reinvigorated by signs of recovery in the economy and increasing numbers of guests slowly returning to the Hotel (Snater, 2015). In early 2010 Mr Snater was predicting an optimistic outlook for the Hotel; *"We have averaged about 24% occupancy over the past few years, but this year it should be close to 50%"* (Hotel & Restaurant Magazine, 2010).

By 2011 tourism was steadily recovering, Mr Snater recording *"we have seen an increase in occupancies from 2010, for all months except March, with July showing a massive 21% increase in occupancy from last year"* (van Winsen, 2011), and the average length of stay grew from 1.1 days in 2009 to 2.4 days in 2012, reflecting recovering confidence in the country as a tourism destination.

The Stables Lounge became the home of the Larry Norton Gallery in May 2009, displaying works by this fine local artist known for his breath-taking African landscapes and wildlife paintings.

Health Hazard

In late 2010 national newspapers reported that raw sewage was being dumped directly into the Zambezi River from the small sewage plant built in the 1950's to handle the Hotel's waste. Tourists had taken photographs of unprocessed sewage waste flowing into the river, and an unnamed local official apparently confirming that due to lack of financial resources raw sewage had been channelled into the river for over a year (Victoria Falls Bits and Blogs, November 2010).

In 2016 the town's Municipality announced a $12 million upgrade to the struggling sewage system (Victoria Falls Bits and Blogs, September 2016).

Conservation Gardening

In March 2012 the Hotel launched a pioneering Eco-Initiative in partnership with Conservation Science Africa helping to develop community-based projects that contribute towards creating a 'clean and resilient Victoria Falls conservation-economy.' The eco-initiative promotes green homestead/village technologies that are efficient, affordable and user friendly, covering waste management, recycling, water usage and renewable energy.

The Hotel launched the initiative with the start of the Conservation Gardening Project, utilising the Hotel's own vegetable gardens to trial and teach conservation tillage practices, including the building of eco-composting wormeries, organic vegetable gardens and rotational crop plot management systems. The project aims to reduce deforestation pressures through the rehabilitation of degraded land and creation of intensive, well managed, high yielding gardens and plots. The Hotel's organic vegetable gardens proudly provide many of the fresh herbs and vegetables used in the Hotel's kitchens.

Mr Togni Takes the Reins

Mr Giulio Togni was appointed General Manager of the Hotel in November 2012, moving from the north bank of the river where he had been manager of The Royal Livingstone Hotel, part of the redevelopment of the old Intercontinental Hotel site on the north bank of the Falls opened by Sun International in 2001.

"As the new General Manager of the Hotel, I am enjoying my stay at this prestigious hospitality institution and look forward to being of service to you and all our guests in coming months and years. Since arriving on November 1st, I have been impressed with all the features of this Hotel - its history, its staff, its guests, its position within the hospitality industry in Southern Africa and the genuine affection with which it is held by so very many people around the world."
(Victoria Falls Hotel, November 2012)

Mr Giulio Togni

Luxury Defined

In January 2013 a $3.5 million refurbishment programme was announced, funded by the Hotel's management partners, African Sun and Meikles. Mr Karl Snater, now Meikles Hospitality Managing Director, oversaw the works, aimed at updating and improving the already high standards of the Hotel. The expertise in design and historic detail was again provided by Mr Graham Viney.

The Livingstone Room

The extensive programme of works scheduled in the first phase included refurbishment of the Livingstone Room, Lounge, Bulawayo and Centenary Rooms, and full refurbishment of the Stables Wing, including all bedrooms and suites.

The refurbishment of the Livingstone Room, the Hotel's flagship dining venue, included the replacement of all carpets, curtains, fans and furniture, with the interior décor developed to opulent standards. A new addition to the room was the arrival of a full sized sixty-year old grand piano.

> *"The recent refurbishment of the Hotel, which included work on The Livingstone Room, was designed to further enhance the venue's attractiveness, and has been matched by on-going efforts to continuously improve service standards and to ensure that the cuisine featured on the menu is of world-class standard. In this regard, we pay tribute in particular to the work being undertaken by our development chef, Mike Ovens, who has brought a wealth of international experience and innovation to the food and beverage operations of the hotel in general and The Livingstone Room in particular."* (Karl Snater, Victoria Falls Hotel, October 2013)

Following refurbishment, the Livingstone Room received several notable awards, including being voted the best hotel restaurant in Africa, seventh overall in the

The Bulawayo Room

world, by The Daily Meal, a highly respected international website concentrating in culinary excellence (Zambezi Traveller, November 2013).

Scottish Chef Mike Ovens expanded in an interview:

> *"We have two wonderful organic herb gardens - which is a chefs dream - to nip out to the garden for fresh herbs just before service, is something chefs all over the world would envy.* [However,] *trying to get a constant supply of quality ingredients can be a challenge. We fly our seafood in from Scotland and a lot of produce is flown in from Johannesburg."* (Victoria Falls Hotel, June 2012)

Included in his notable speciality dishes were pork terrine with crocodile and black pudding, beef wellington with wild mushroom duxelle, and hand-dived Scottish king scallops.

A 'soft refurbishment' - the complete replacement and upgrading of furniture and fittings - was undertaken in the Lounge, Bulawayo and Centenary Rooms.

The stand-alone Stables Wing underwent a full refurbishment, including converting

Stables Wing Bedroom

the rooms to doubles with King-size beds. At the conclusion of the works the wing was re-branded and re-launched as the Stables Signature Wing. As part of the higher standard of services the wing now offered private check-in services in the Stables Lounge, butler service, complimentary massage and valet service. The Hotel's manager, Giulio Togni, recorded:

"These 42 deluxe rooms, all of the same superior standard, provide an ambiance of exclusive luxury with special elements such as private check-in and lounge, afternoon tea and pastries and a complimentary massage voucher. This is virtually a hotel within a hotel." (Victoria Falls Hotel, June 2015)

Redesigning and soft refurbishment was also undertaken of the deluxe suites in the North and South Hammerhead Wings, including enlarging the rooms, remodelling the private lounge and bathroom areas and replacement of furniture and fittings. The upgrades included the installation of mini bars and flat-screen televisions in all 161 rooms and suites.

Changes on the Terrace included extensive refurbishment and expansion, including the relocation of Stanley's Bar onto the Terrace. In addition a larger upgraded kitchen was planned to service the Terrace.

The Larry Norton Gallery

The Pool Pavilion underwent refurbishment, the old service bar converted into a relaxing loggia with open plan arches, extensive tiling and Moroccan styled interior.

The Larry Norton Gallery relocated from the Stables Lounge to its present location in the Palm Lounge in April 2014.

Pullman Suite Reborn

After being redeveloped as a luxury shop and gallery in 1996, the Pullman Suite was reinstated and reopened in 2013.

> *"The Pullman Suite is imposing, with an elegant style and emphasis on comfort and class reflected in the teak and leather finishes of furnishings. In contrast to this is a range of modern technology and equipment... to give recognition to 21st century needs."* (Zambezi Traveller, March 2014)

The room caters for up to 40 people conference style, or can be used boardroom style for up to 25 delegates and a secretarial service is operated by the Hotel.

The Pullman Suite

Century Plus Ten

The 110th anniversary of the Hotel, promoted under the 'Century Plus 10' banner, was celebrated with a week of events in June 2014. The celebrations culminated in a special event held in the Livingstone Room, where one hundred and ten selected guests toasted one hundred and ten years of first class service.

Hosted by Mr Togni, the Hotel's General Manager, and Mr Snater, Meikles Hospitality Managing Director, guests included Minister of Tourism and Hospitality, Walter Mzembi. Mr Togni announced:

"As we celebrate this Century Plus 10, as we have called it, we have re-affirmed our commitment to excellence in all that we do and to hosting, on behalf of Zimbabwe and all Zimbabweans, guests from all over the world." (Zambezi Traveller, March 2014)

The event also celebrated long serving staff at the Hotel, including Mr Dorman Marapata, Mr Duly Chitimbire, Mr Philip Mulenga and most notably Mr Phillip

The Curio Shop and Ndau Collection display in the Hotel Reception

James, Restaurants Manager, for over 45 years of loyal and diligent service - the Hotel's longest serving member of staff, having joined the Hotel in 1968.

A new addition in the Reception Hall was the opening in June 2014 of The Ndau Collection displays, joining the Victoria Falls Hotel Shop. A Victoria Falls based company, Ndau specialise in fine sterling silver jewellery influenced by Africa's rich cultural and natural history.

Centre Stage

In August 2013 the Hotel hosted the opening reception of the 20th Session of the United Nations World Tourism Organisation General Assembly, jointly hosted by the towns of Livingstone and Victoria Falls. The event attracted more than a thousand delegates and V.I.P. guests from across the world and provided a significant boost to local tourism, as well as giving Zimbabwe valuable international marketing exposure.

In their inaugural addresses, President Robert Mugabe of Zimbabwe and President Michael Sata of Zambia called for increased support for sustainable tourism and development that improves the welfare and livelihoods of local communities.

Addressing delegates at the opening session, the U.N.W.T.O. Secretary General, Taleb Rifai, underscored the event as a *"timely opportunity for all of us to continue along an encouraging path to drive tourism towards its fullest potential in fostering sustainable economic growth, jobs and development, and what better backdrop to do so than here in Africa, a region where we believe tourism can be a true force for good"*

The Bridge illuminated

The UNWTO Secretary General declared:

"This is the best attended General Assembly in the history of the organization. This session saw participation from 121 full delegates from member states, 140 delegates from all over the world, and 750 other delegates, 900 delegates from the media and the private sector and 49 foreign ministers." (UNWTO, 2014)

With unprecedented numbers of guests gathered on the front lawns, the Hotel overcame many logistical challenges to lay on an event that was commended for its smooth operation, excellent food and a dream location. As nightfall gathered the Victoria Falls Bridge was illuminated as part of a new installation celebrating the joint event. One of the Australian delegates commented:

"A genuine treat to be hosted by this grand, historic Hotel in what must be one of the finest settings for a social gathering on the entire African continent." (Higgins, 2015)

Stamp of Approval

Developments in 2015, the Hotel's 111th year of operation, included the opening

New Courtyard entrance into the Livingstone Room

of a new entrance for the Livingstone Room from the central Courtyard, featuring French windows and columned veranda.

Tourism arrivals to Victoria Falls remained around 200,000 a year, with tourism negatively affected by the shadow of Ebola, even though the epidemic did not directly affect the southern African region.

2015 postage stamp

An illustration of the Hotel featured on a postage stamp, part of a set of four featuring historical hotels, issued in 2015. Other hotels in the set included the Bulawayo Club, Meikles Hotel (Harare) and Leopard Rock Hotel (Eastern Highlands).

Going Green

Tourism operators in the Falls have in recent years increasingly adopted positive 'eco-tourism' principles, aiming to minimise environmental impacts and supporting conservation and community initiatives in the local area. In early 2016 several leading accommodation providers, including the Victoria Falls Hotel, partnered with Green-Tourism.com in a trial project to encourage industry adoption of sustainable eco-tourism management practices.

Victoria Falls Airport Expands

A new chapter in travel and transport to the Victoria Falls began in April 2013 with the commencement of significant $150 million redevelopment and expansion of the Victoria Falls International Airport, partially opened at the end of 2015 and officially opened by President Robert Mugabe on 18th November 2016. Works included the construction of an extended four kilometre runway and associated taxiways, the construction of new terminal buildings with air-traffic control tower and supporting emergency services.

The new airport runway, expanded from a length of 2,200 metres to 4,000 metres and doubled in width to 60 metres, and will allow international travellers to fly directly to Victoria Falls, accommodating the Boeing 747 and new generation of wide-bodied aircraft. The new terminal building has been designed to handle 1.2 million international travellers (compared to the previous capacity of 400,000) and 500,000 domestic passengers per annum. Concerns have been expressed,

The new terminal buildings under construction (May 2015)

however, on the associated impact of increased tourism numbers, with pressure to develop new accommodation and concerns over the visitor carrying capacity of the Rainforest during peak-season (Roberts, 2021b).

National tourist arrivals increased to 2,422,930 in 2017 from 2,167,686 in 2016. Victoria Falls' 'big ten' accommodation providers reported a 18.5 percent increase in hotel occupancy across the year, with an additional 35,730 tourist room nights sold. The ten main tourism hotels in the resort now offered a combined total of 1,125 rooms across the resort.

The increase in arrivals was largely credited to the expanded Victoria Falls International Airport, which has seen traditional carriers increasing their capacity and welcomed three new international airlines to serve the destination - creating an additional 127,000 passenger seats into Victoria Falls per annum (Victoria Falls Bits and Blogs, January 2018).

Business As Usual

In late November 2017 Emmerson Mnangagwa became Zimbabwe's third President since Independence, ousting his aging predecessor, Robert Mugabe in a bloodless coup d' état. After winning national elections President Mnangagwa was officially inaugurated in August 2018 with the new administration's adopted mantra, 'Zimbabwe is Open for Business,' aimed to encouraging foreign investment and development. A wave of optimism spread through the tourism sector, hoping for a resurgence in international arrivals at the resort and stimulating a cascade of investment into new and existing hotel and lodge developments around the town, including the planned construction of several new luxury hotels.

In late 2018 a significant refurbishment programme was announced at the Falls Hotel, with plans also initiated to enlarge the Hotel in the near future.

"A refurbishment programme for the Victoria Falls Hotel will commence before the end of 2018. However, of greater significance is a project to enlarge the Hotel with additional accommodation which is currently in the initial stages of planning." (Victoria Falls Bits and Blogs, July 2018)

National arrivals increased again for 2018, reaching a new record high of 2,579,974, with the country's tourism industry targeting an ambitious 3,000,000 arrivals for 2019 (Victoria Falls Bits and Blogs, May 2019). The year was, however, a difficult one for the tourism industry, mainly attributed to issues on negative destination image. National tourist arrivals fell by 11 percent to 2.29 million.

Rise to the Top

Mr Farai H Chimba became the latest General Manager of the Hotel in May 2019 after serving over six years as the Hotel's Deputy General Manager. Zimbabwean by birth, Mr Chimba joined the Meikles Hotel in Harare in 2000, holding the positions of Resident Manager and Food and Beverage Manager. Mr Chimba was seconded to The Victoria Falls Hotel Partnership as Food and Beverage Manager in August 2008 to spearhead the revitalizing of the Food and Beverage experience.

Front view of Hotel showing Stanley's Bar and Terrace

Regeneration and Renewal

In November 2019 the Hotel announced the two-year refurbishment programme planned to being in 2020:

"The updates focus on increasing comfort and luxury for the modern traveller, while improving on flexibility, creating 'Classic' rooms and family accommodation, and updating some of the suites. When the project is complete, the Victoria Falls Hotel will have 61 Classic rooms, two of which will be Classic Access rooms, 7 Family rooms, 25 Premium rooms, 11 Suites, 42 Stables Signature Wing rooms (which are already existing and will not be changed) - bringing the total to 148 bedrooms from the current 161 rooms.

"Key features of the exercise will be increasing the inflow of light, granting greater access to the views of the Hotel grounds, creating walk-in showers in bathrooms, as well as upgrading lighting, air conditioning and electrical features such as points for using and charging devices in all bedrooms and suites. The aesthetic thrust will be achieved with use of new structural features and in the use of colour, furnishings, ornaments and basic decor." (Victoria Falls Bits and Blogs, November 2019)

Subsequent events would see the start of the redevelopment programme suspended until April 2021.

View of the front of the Hotel from the veranda

Global Pandemic

Global events overtook the tourist destination in early 2020 with fears over the widespread transmission of the new coronavirus leading to the World Health Organisation announcing a global pandemic on 11th March 2020. Tourism operators and hoteliers in Victoria Falls announced a voluntary suspension of operations at the end of March after mass cancellations of bookings brought hotel occupancy levels down to single digit figures.

With a large percentage of the town's workforce unemployed due to the crisis, the Hotel supported efforts to help the local community through the national lockdown that followed, the Hotel's nursery providing a large number of seedlings as part of a 'Feed Your Community' gardening campaign and supporting a project providing regular daily meals to the town's school children. By the end of the year the scheme had served over half a million meals, funded entirely by donations and supported by local tourism operators and community initiatives (Roberts, 2021b).

The Victoria Falls Hotel reopened at the end of the year to limited domestic tourism over the festive season. With national lockdowns and international travel restrictions and throughout the world, the Hotel's Deputy General Manager, Mr Temba Maripakwenda, announced a significant shift in the Hotel's target audience.

"The Hotel has slashed accommodation and meals rates by more than half to cater for the domestic market in line with country's drive to promote domestic tourism. Our guests are happy so far because of our competitive rates. We are a five-star Hotel and you can't find such discounts anywhere. We have all... [the necessary] Covid-19 protocols in place and our staff has been trained hence guests are assured of their safety and protection." (Victoria Falls Bits and Blogs, December 2020)

Very sadly one long standing and well loved member of the Hotel's staff team, Mr Phillip James, its longest serving member of staff, passed away during the year.

Global international travel restrictions continued into 2021. In early 2021 the Hotel announced the opening of a dedicated on-site emergency medical clinic with nurse care and on-call doctors, oxygen facilities, blood pressure monitoring and basic health check-up and support equipment, along with Covid-19 testing for guests of the Hotel.

Yesterday, Today and Tomorrow

The Victoria Falls Hotel has become one of the best-known and most highly regarded hospitality establishments in Africa, joining an elite group of hotels with a global profile, and being associated with other famous names such as Raffles in Singapore or the Mount Nelson in Cape Town.

From its early humble railway beginnings the Hotel has grown and evolved into a tourism icon, known alongside the great natural wonder of the Falls and overlooking the man-made engineering marvel of the Victoria Falls Bridge. Known to generations of travellers the Hotel has survived fluctuating fortunes, risen to fashionable heights and suffered from challenging lows, through changing political and economic uncertainties, evolving transportation methods and shifting global tourism trends.

The oldest operating hotel in Zimbabwe, the building has taken on an identity of its own, 'The Grand Old Lady of the Falls,' matriarch of the Victoria Falls tourism industry. The corridors of the Hotel play testimony to this rich heritage with vintage travel posters, memorabilia of Royal visits and period photographs of ages past.

The magnificent Msasa tree on the front lawns

Unchallenged in her position for the first fifty years, the Hotel now competes with a multitude of hotels on both sides of the river, yet none can claim to rival her pedigree or prestige. For over the a century the Hotel has played a central role in the development of tourism at the Falls, as well as the small town which has grown up around it, and has become firmly established as the one of the Leading Hotels of the World.

The Hotel currently has a total of 161 rooms, divided into 69 standard rooms (nine of which are inter-leading), 40 Central deluxe rooms, 42 Stable Signature Rooms, two honeymoon suites, two deluxe suites, two executive suites, and the Batoka, Presidential and Royal Suites. Guest services include complimentary wi-fi services throughout the Hotel, Internet Lounge, Hair Salon, Beauty Spa, Gym/Fitness room, and same day dry-cleaning and valet services.

And yet whilst the never ending waves of change continue, some things do stay the same. No longer a victim of fashions and trends, the Hotel has evolved a style of its own, reflecting a romantic vision of the past and the timeless charm of days gone by with the all the luxury and convenience of the modern world, all encapsulated within its buildings, rooms and corridors.

The subtle scent of 'Yesterday, today and tomorrow' flowers drifts on the gentle breeze from the gardens, a reminder of the rich tapestry of nature which surrounds the Hotel. Baboons continue to give the Hotel groundsmen the daily run-around, some even venturing into the Hotel corridors to raid the room-service trolleys for milk and sugar. Foraging warthog families dig up the verdant lawns and mud-bathe in the flower beds, and the nocturnal chirping of frogs and croaking of toads from the courtyard ponds probably still keeps the occasional guest awake late into the night. But after all, what would one expect in the heart of Africa?

Acknowledgements

I am indebted to many people for their help and assistance in the production of this book. Special thanks go to Gail van Jaarsveldt and the Jafuta Foundation (www.jafutafoundation.org) for commissioning and supporting the research and publication of the first edition of this book.

Thanks go to Gordon Murray of the Bulawayo Railway Museum, for his assistance and access to the railway archives under his responsibility. I am also grateful to George S Mudenda, Director of the Livingstone Museum and his dedicated staff for their support, including Perrice Nkombwe and Kingsley Choongo.

I am especially indebted to the work of John Creewel, Manager of the Hotel during the early 1980s, and who sadly died in a car accident in the early 1990s. Mr Creewel gathered extensive material on the history of the Hotel, published posthumously in 1994 as '90 Glorious Years, a History of the Victoria Falls Hotel,' and updated by Stan Higgins ten years later as '100 Years.' The material he collected was donated to the Hotel by his wife, Jeanette, and now forms the core of the Hotel's historical archive - and an invaluable source of references used in this book. Special thanks also go to Jeanette Creewel for her comments and support.

My appreciation goes to Giulio Togni, General Manager of the Hotel, and his staff, notably Sindiso Mabhena and Phillip James, for their help and assistance whilst accommodating me at the beginning of this historical odyssey in late 2014. Thanks also go to Farai Chimba, the current Manager of the Hotel for his help with this revised edition.

Three other key individuals, Karl Snater, Graham Viney and Stan Higgins, all with long associations with the Hotel, are especially thanked for their patience, support and assistance, over many emails, as are also Mark Jones, Manager of the Hotel in the 1980s, and Christopher Jarrett, Assistant Manager at the Hotel in the early 1970s.

Special thanks also go to those who share an interest in the history of the Victoria Falls for access to their precious archive reference material, knowledge and support, including David Moir, Hugh Macmillan, Peter Jones, Graham Andrews, Larry Cumming, Larry Norton and again, Gail van Jaarsveldt. Bryony Rheam assisted with information on Agatha Christie's visit to the Hotel in 1922.

Many of the historical photographs used are from the railway archives held in the Bulawayo Railway Museum, taken by unnamed publicity photographers over the years and digitally copied by the author. Some of the early images were taken by Percy Clark, and the photographs on page 4, 10, 165 and from 174 onwards are by the author, largely taken over the last couple of years, with the exception of the image of Mr Togni on page 194, which is used with thanks. Special thanks go to Gordon Shepherd/Stenlake Publishing for the use of the image on page 45 and Dr Anthony Klein for the use of the image on page 164.

Thanks also go to the Elephant Walk Shopping and Artists Village (www. elephantswalk.com) and Travellers Guest House (www.travellerszim.net) for accommodating me during visits to Victoria Falls and Bulawayo, and likewise others too many to mention on both sides of the river, for their hospitality and friendship over many visits over many years.

Final and biggest thanks go to family and friends for their support, help and advice during the development of this book.

1905 advert for the Hotel

References

Three primary archive libraries for references are indicated; the archives of the Bulawayo Railway Museum (Zimbabwe), identified as 'BRMA' in the reference list, the archive collection of the Livingstone Museum (Zambia), labelled 'LM', and the private collection of the late Mr John Creewel, known as the Creewel Collection and now forming the core of the Hotel's own archive, identified as 'CC.'

Aberman, G. (1955) Africa's Famous Hotel, Holiday & Travel Magazine, June/July. Salisbury, Southern Rhodesia. [CC]

Adelaide Chronicle (August 1925) Monsters of Africa. 22 August 1925. [Online source: https://trove.nla.gov.au/newspaper/article/89631044]

Agate, W. (1912) Diary of a tour in South Africa. Holness, London.

American Dental Journal (1906). The Dental Summary. Vol.26, No.5, p.229.

Anon (undated) Recollections from the Victoria Falls Hotel, 1930s [CC]

Balfour, H. (1905) Diaries of Henry Balfour (1863-1939) South Africa 1905 [Online source: www.prm.ox.ac.uk/south-africa-july-december-1905]

Balfour, H. (1929) Diaries of Henry Balfour (1863-1939) South and East Africa 1929. [Online source: www.prm.ox.ac.uk/south-and-east-africa-1929-tour-president-anthropology-section-baas-british-association-advancement]

Baxter T. W. and Clay, G. (1963) The Discovery And Historical Associations [In Fagan, B. M. [Editor] (1963), Chapter 1.]

Bell, J. (2020) Personal communications with author, August 2020.

Black, C. (1976) The Legend of Lomagundi. North-Western Development Association, Southern Rhodesia.

Blake, W. T. (1960) Rhodesia and Nyasaland Journey. Redman, London.

Brisbane Telegraph (November 1906) Brighton on the Zambesi. 20th November.

British South Africa Annual (1916-7) The New Victoria Falls Hotel, p97-99 [CC]

British South Africa Company (1905) Annual Report [CC]

British South Africa Company (1907) Rhodesia, A Book for Tourists and Sportsmen.

Bulawayo Chronicle (May 1904) For Visitors to the Falls. 7th May.

Bulawayo Chronicle (June 1904) Victoria Falls Hotel. 4th June.

Bulawayo Chronicle (July 1904) Victoria Falls Hotel notice. 9th July.

Bulawayo Chronicle (October 1904) A Trip to the Falls. 15th October.

Bulawayo Chronicle (August 1905a) Livingstone Notes. 26th August.

Bulawayo Chronicle (September 1906) Advert, The Grand Hotel. 9th September.

Bulawayo Chronicle (April 1909) N-W R Notes - The Heavy Rains. 9th April.

Bulawayo Chronicle (October 1909) Through Rhodesia - A Visitor's Impressions.

15th October.

Bulawayo Chronicle (June 2910) The Gaiety Co's Concert. 24th June.

Bulawayo Chronicle (April 1958a) No sale of Falls Hotel yet. 10th April.

Bulawayo Chronicle (April 1958b) Panic to cash our assets. 15th April.

Bulawayo Chronicle (September 1958) Falls Hotel not for sale. 26th September.

Bulawayo Chronicle (May 1959) Fewer visitors at Victoria Falls Hotel. 30th May.

Cameron, C. (1913) A Woman's Winter in Africa. Stanley Paul & Co, London.

Caterer & Hotelkeeper Magazine (1982) Crocodile cocktail was star turn in Zimbabwe. 4th November 1982. p.36. London. [CC]

Caterer & Hotelkeeper Magazine (1984) Zimbabwe's oldest tourist hotel celebrates 80 years. 4th April. p.38. London. [CC]

Chappell, I. (2020) The racism I have seen in cricket. [Online source: www. espncricinfo.com/story/_/id/29340851/my-experience-racism-cricket]

Clark, P. M. (1936) Autobiography of an Old Drifter. Harrap, London.

Corner, C. (undated) Photograph album. Private collection.

Cosmopolitan (1962) Unknown article, Vol.152, p.25 [Online source: https://books. google.co.uk/books?id=Sc1ZAAAAYAAJ]

Cowen, W. W. (1995) A Central African Odyssey. Radcliffe Press.

Creewel, J. (2004) A history of the Victoria Falls Hotel - 100 years 1904-2004. Edited and updated by Stan Higgins. (Originally published in 1994 as A history of the Victoria Falls Hotel - 90 Glorious Years 1904-1994).

Creewel, J. & Shiels, D. (1999) A brief history of the Victoria Falls Hotel. [Guest Information leaflet, Victoria Falls Hotel]

Critchell, R. (2007) A Visiting Fireman in Africa. [Online source: www. greatnorthroad.org/boma/Fireman_in_Africa]

Croxton, A. H. (1982) Railways of Zimbabwe (Originally published in 1973 as Railways of Rhodesia).

Fagan, B, M. [Editor] (1963) The Victoria Falls : A Handbook to the Victoria Falls, the Batoka Gorge, and part of the Upper Zambesi River. Lusaka.

Flight Magazine (1929) Eddies. 28th February, p162. [Online source: www. flightglobal.com/pdfarchive/view/1929/1929%20-%200404.html]

Flight Magazine (1951) Not-so-dark Africa. 5th October. p.446 [Online source: www.flightglobal.com/pdfarchive/view/1951/1951%20-%202003.html]

Frew, A. A. (1934) Prince George's African Tour. Blackie & Sons.

Green, L. G. (1968) Full Many a Glorious Morning. Timmins.

Gregg, L. (1957) Memories of Olive Schreiner. W & R Chambers, London.

Hardman, R. (2018) Queen of the World, The Global Biography. Penguin Books.

Harris, D. (1969) Victoria Falls Souvenir Guide Book.

Henderson (undated) Recollections of the visit of Dr Henderson, 1933 [CC]

Hensman, H. (1901) Cecil Rhodes A Study. William Blackwood and Sons.

Higgins, S. (2015) Personal communications with author, November 2015.

Hobson, G. (1923) The Great Zambezi Bridge - The Story of a Famous Engineering Feat. [In Weinthal, L. (Editor) 1923. The Story of the Cape to Cairo Railway and River Route from 1887–1922. Pioneer Publishing Co.

Hotel & Catering Magazine (1984) 80th Anniversary for Vic Falls Hotel [CC]

Hotel & Restaurant Magazine (2010) Vic Falls reports an upswing in arrivals. [Online source: http://www.hotelandrestaurant.co.za/tourism/vic-falls-hotel-aims-to-double-occupancy/]

James, D. (1954) The Life of Lord Roberts. Hollis & Carter.

Jarrett, C. (2015) Personal communications with author, November 2015.

Jones, M. C. (2015) Personal communications with author, November 2015.

Kalgoorlie Miner (June 1934) Devil of the Cataract. 5th June 1934 [Online source: https://trove.nla.gov.au/newspaper/article/95035527]

Kernan, K. (1984) Personal communication with J Creewel, 4th March 1985 [CC]

Kondor, L. (1990) The Seaman's Trunk - A Real-life Mystery of the Victoria Falls. Africa Calls Magazine, May/June 1990.

Livingstone, D. (1857) Missionary travels and researches in South Africa. London.

Livingstone Mail (April 1906) 21st April. No.3 (Quoted in Arrington, 2010).

Livingstone Mail (August 1906) Victoria Falls Notes, No.19. 4th August. [LM]

Livingstone Mail (October 1906) Unfortunate Accident at Victoria Falls, No.30. 20th October. [LM]

Livingstone Mail (December 1906) Livingstone in 1906 - A Retrospect. Christmas Edition. December. [LM]

Livingstone Mail (January 1907) Meeting with His Honour the Administrator, No.43. 19th January. [LM]

Livingstone Mail (February 1908) Mr Holland's Farewell Banquet, No.98. 8th February. [LM]

Livingstone Mail (May 1908) Victoria Falls Hotel, No.112. 16th May. [LM]

Livingstone Mail (March 1909) Front page advertisement for the North-Western Hotel. 13th March. No.155. [LMA]

Livingstone Mail (April 1909) Notes and Mems, No.161. 24th April. [LM]

Lyon, P. (1904) The Arderne Party Chronicles. Cape Town.

McAdams, J. (1969) Birth of an Airline - Establishment of Rhodesian and Nyasaland Airways [Online source: www.rhodesia.nl/Aviation/rana.htm]

McGregor, J. (2009) Crossing the Zambezi : The Politics of Landscape on an African Frontier.

McNeil, D. G. (1997) Expeditions; Revisiting the Empire, but Just for Design. New York Times, 9th October 1997. [Online source: www.nytimes.com/1997/10/09/garden/expeditions-revisiting-the-empire-but-just-for-design]

Martin, D. (1997) Victoria Falls: Mosi-oa-Tunya African Publishing Group, Harare.

Meadows, K. (2000) Sometimes When It Rains: White Africans in Black Africa. Thorntree Press.

Melbourne Argus (January 1934) Monster in Zambesi. 13th January [Online source: https://trove.nla.gov.au/newspaper/article/11729228]

Metcalfe, Sir C, and Richarde-Seaver, Major F. I. (1889) The British Sphere of Influence in South Africa. Fortnightly Review, Vol.267, p.351-63. London.

Metcalfe, Sir C. (1904) Cape to Cairo Railway. Dawson Daily News, 29th September 1904. [Online source: https://news.google.com/newspapers?nid=41&dat=19040922&id=TJ4jAAAAIBAJ&sjid=1DYDAAAAIBAJ&pg=4126,6068996&hl=en]

Moore, J. (2012) Hotels at War [Online source: www.rhodesianassociation.com/armies-that-served-rhodesia]

Morrah, D. (1947) The Royal Family in Africa, Hutchinson.

Northern Rhodesia Journal (July 1953) Island Names. Vol.2, No.2, p.89.

Northern Rhodesia Journal (January 1956) A Country in Search of a Name. J. A. Gray. Vol.3, No.1, p.75-78.

Northern Rhodesia Journal (January 1959) Kalomo - Livingstone in 1907. L. B. Hunt. Vol.4, No.1, p.9-17.

Northern Rhodesia Journal (July 1959) Recollections of Piet Erasmus. Vol.4, No.2, p.159-165.

Palin, M. (1992) Pole to Pole, BBC Books, London.

Perth Western Mail (February 1915) The Victoria Falls, Zambesi. A. V. Fuller. 8th February 1915 [Online source: https://trove.nla.gov.au/newspaper/article/44753900]

Phillipson, D. W. [Editor] (1990) Mosi-oa-Tunya: a handbook to the Victoria Falls region. Salisbury: Longman, Zimbabwe. (First Published, 1975)

Price, J. H. (1966) Behind the Headlines, Modern Tramway and Light Railway Review. Vol.29 No.338 p.48-49.

Price, W. (1962) Incredible Africa. John Day Company, New York.

Prichard, M. [Editor] (2013) The Grand Tour: Around the World with the Queen of Mystery. Harper Collins.

Reserve Bank of Zimbabwe (2015) Demonetization of the Zimbabwe Dollar. [Online source: http://www.rbz.co.zw/assets/demonetisation-press-statement-9-june-2015.pdf]

Rhodesia Railways (1905) Minutes of Ordinary General Meeting [CC]

Rhodesia Railways (March 1956) Letter from Ministry of Transport, Victoria Falls Hotel: Supplies. 20th March. [BRMA, unpublished]

Rhodesia Railways (August 1956a) Letter from Acting General Manager, Victoria Falls Hotel: Supplies. 6th August. [BRMA, unpublished]

Rhodesia Railways (August 1956b) Letter from Acting General Manager, Victoria Falls Hotel: Catering for Asiatics. 10th August. [BRMA, unpublished]

Rhodesia Railways (July 1957) Letter from Ministry of Transport and Communications, The Victoria Falls Hotel. 15th July. [BRMA, unpublished]

Rhodesia Railways (November 1957) Minutes of the one hundred and fourth Board Meeting of the Rhodesia Railways. 26th November. [BRMA, unpublished]

Rhodesia Railways (June 1958) Letter from Secretary, Victoria Falls Hotel. 27th June. [BRMA, unpublished]

Rhodesia Railways (January 1959) Letter from Acting General Manager, Victoria Falls Hotel. 6th January. [BRMA, unpublished]

Rhodesia Railways (June 1959a) Letter from Ministry of Transport. 4th June. [BRMA, unpublished]

Rhodesia Railways (June 1959b) Letter from General Manager, Memorandum on the Victoria Falls Hotel. 20th June. [BRMA, unpublished]

Rhodesia Railways (August 1959) Letter from General Manager to Rhodesia Railways Board Secretary, August 1959 [BRMA, unpublished]

Rhodesia Railways (March 1960) Letter from Secretary for Local Government. 30th March. [BRMA, unpublished]

Rhodesia Railways, (April 1960) Letter from General Manager, Proposal to lease the Victoria Falls Hotel to private enterprise. 8th April. [BRMA, unpublished]

Rhodesia Railways (March 1961) Letter from Vice-Chairman of Rhodesia Railways Board. 7th March. [BRMA, unpublished]

Rhodesia Railways (November 1961) Railway Board Capital Expenditure Form. 21st November. [BRMA, unpublished]

Rhodesia Railways (February 1963) Letter from General Manager, Memorandum on the Victoria Falls Hotel. 19th February. [BRMA, unpublished]

Rhodesia Railways (March 1963) Memo from General Manager, The Victoria Falls

Hotel: Progress Report. 26th March. [BRMA, unpublished]

Rhodesia Railways (May 1963) Minutes of 11th meeting of The Victoria Falls Management Committee. 11th May. [BRMA, unpublished]

Rhodesia Railways (April 1964) Memo, The Victoria Falls Hotel: Capital Improvements. 24th April. [BRMA, unpublished]

Rhodesia Railways (August 1964) Report from Mr Schefftel, The Victoria Falls Hotel, preliminary survey report. 17th August. [BRMA, unpublished]

Rhodesia Railways (October 1964) Letter from the Chief Civil Engineer. 1st October. [BRMA, unpublished]

Rhodesia Railways (November 1964) Letter from the Architect, Report on position of programme for improvements required at the Victoria Falls Hotel. 30th November. [BRMA, unpublished]

Rhodesia Railways (March 1965) Letter from the Chairman, Rhodesia Railways. 26th March. [BRMA, unpublished]

Rhodesia Railways Bulletin (April 1929) History of the strike. No.31, p.11-13.

Rhodesia Railways Bulletin (May 1931) Extension to Victoria Falls Hotel. No.52, p.10-11.

Rhodesia Railways Bulletin (March 1934) Visit of H.R.H. Prince George. No.87, p.1-3.

Rhodesia Railways Bulletin (July 1934) Value for Money. No.90, p.1173.

Rhodesia Railways Bulletin (November 1938) The Victoria Falls Hotel. No.142, p.15-17.

Rhodesia Railways Bulletin (April 1947) The Royal Visit. No.177, p1-7.

Rhodesia Railways Bulletin (March 1949) The world visits the Victoria Falls. No.200, p.9.

Rhodesia Railways Bulletin (February 1950) Extensions to the Victoria Falls Hotel. No.211, p.14-15.

Rhodesia Railways Bulletin (June 1950) Juvenile high spirits. No.215, p.8.

Rhodesia Railways Bulletin (February 1951) The railways as caterers. No.223, p.6.

Rhodesia Railways Magazine (May 1952) District notes, Victoria Falls. Vol.1, No.1, p.36.

Rhodesia Railways Magazine (June 1952) District notes, Victoria Falls. Vol.1, No.2, p.27.

Rhodesia Railways Magazine (July 1952) District notes, Victoria Falls. Vol.1, No.3, p.27.

Rhodesia Railways Magazine (December 1954) First Hotel Built in a Month. Vol.3, No.8, p.13.

Rhodesia Railways Magazine (March 1955) Three parties of world tourists visit the Falls, Vol.3, No.11, p.11.

Rhodesia Railways Magazine (April 1955a) Business house had own Falls Special back in 1911. Vol.3 No.12, p.19.

Rhodesia Railways Magazine (April 1955b) Victoria Falls District Notes. Vol.3, No.12, p.34.

Rhodesia Railways Magazine (August 1955) Fifty Years - The Story of a Bridge (Part 2). Vol.4, No.3, p.21-23.

Rhodesia Railways Magazine (March 1956) Caronia Cameos - They Came, They Saw, They Wondered. Vol.4, No.11, p.25.

Rhodesia Railways Magazine (November 1957) Road and Rail Travel in the Good Old Days. Vol.6, No.7, p.33.

Rhodesia Railways Magazine (September 1958) Reminiscences of The Early Days at the Falls. Vol.7, No.5, p.27.

Rhodesia Railways Magazine (July 1961) The Four Corners of the World. Vol.10, No.3, p.17.

Rhodesia Railways Magazine (March 1962) The Falls Fifty Years Ago. Vol.10, No.11, p.15-17.

Rhodesia Railways Magazine (August 1963) Falls Conference. Vol.12, No.4, p.11.

Rhodesia Railways Magazine (December 1964) District notes, Victoria Falls. Vol.13, No.8, p.41.

Rhodesia Railways Magazine (January 1965) District notes, Victoria Falls. Vol.13, No.9, p.44.

Rhodesia Railways Magazine (February 1965) District notes, Victoria Falls. Vol.13, No.10, p.41.

Rhodesia Railways Magazine (June 1965) District notes, Victoria Falls. Vol.14, No.2, p.45.

Rhodesia Railways Magazine (December 1965) District notes, Victoria Falls. Vol.14, No.8, p.51.

Rhodesia Railways Magazine (February 1966) District notes, Victoria Falls. Vol.14, No.10, p.41.

Rhodesia Railways Magazine (July 1966) District notes, Victoria Falls. Vol.15, No.3, p.40.

Rhodesia Railways Magazine (April 1967) District notes, Victoria Falls. Vol.15, No.12, p.44.

Rhodesia Railways Magazine (May 1967) District notes, Victoria Falls. Vol.16, No.1, p.42.

Rhodesia Railways Magazine (October 1967) A Message from the General Manager. Vol.16, No.6, p.4.

Rhodesia Railways Magazine (November 1967) District notes, Victoria Falls. Vol.16, No.7, p.41.

Rhodesia Railways Magazine (March 1970) Railways and Breweries conclude negotiations for the leasing of The Victoria Falls Hotel. Vol.18, No.11, p.12.

Roberts, P. (2020a) Life and Death at the Old Drift, Victoria Falls (1898-1905). Second Edition. Zambezi Book Company / CreateSpace Independent Publishing (First published 2018).

Roberts, P. (2020b) Sun, Steel & Spray - A History of the Victoria Falls Bridge. Third Edition. Zambezi Book Company / CreateSpace Independent Publishing (First published 2011, Victoria Falls Bridge Company, Zimbabwe).

Roberts, P. (2021a) To the Banks of the Zambezi and Beyond - Railway Construction from the Cape to the Congo (1893-1910). First Edition. Zambezi Book Company / CreateSpace Independent Publishing.

Roberts, P. (2021b) Footsteps Through Time - A History of Travel and Tourism to the Victoria Falls. Second Edition. Zambezi Book Company / CreateSpace Independent Publishing (First published 2017).

Scientific American Magazine (1905) Completion of the Victoria Falls Bridge. 22nd July, 1905, p.68-69.

Schoonover, T. R. (1952) T. R. Schoonover's Africa-India Travelogue. [Online source: www.caronia2.info/trs06.php]

Shepherd, G. (2008) Old Livingstone and Victoria Falls. Stenlake Publishing.

Snater, K. (2015) Personal communications with author, November 2015.

South Africa Handbook No.32 (1905) How to Reach the Victoria Falls.p.27. Winchester House, London.

South Africa Handbook No.34 (1905) A Trip to the Victoria Falls and Rhodesia. Winchester House, London.

Southern Rhodesia Publicity Office (1938) The Victoria Falls of Southern Rhodesia. Government Stationery Office.

Stewart, A. D. (2010) Gavuzzo & Gavuzzi: the history of a Piedmontese family from the Middle Ages to the twentieth century. Amelia, Italy 2010.

Strage, M. (1973) Cape to Cairo. Jonathan Cape.

Sykes, F. W. (1905) Official Guide to the Victoria Falls. Bulawayo.

Teede, J. and Teede, F. (1994) African Thunder - The Victoria Falls. Zimbabwe.

The Canberra Times (November 1976) Attack on Motel. Monday 1st November 1976. [Online source: https://trove.nla.gov.au/newspaper/article/131793204]

The Canberra Times (December 1977a) 8 people wounded in shelling. Tuesday 20th December 1977. [Online source: https://trove.nla.gov.au/newspaper/article/110883647]

The Canberra Times (December 1977b) Tourist resort shelled again. Tuesday

27th December 1977. [Online source: https://trove.nla.gov.au/newspaper/article/110884615]

The Sydney Sun (December 1949) Victoria Falls Are Almost Dehydrated. 27th December 1949. [Online source: https://trove.nla.gov.au/newspaper/article/230741817]

The Worlds Work (February 1905). Among the World's Wonders. Vol.9 No.4, p.5879.

UNWTO (2014) UNWTO General Assembly Opens. [Online source: www.zw.one.un.org/newsroom/news/untwo-general-assembly-opens]

Varian, H. F. (1953) Some African Milestones. Oxford.

Victoria Falls Bits and Blogs (November 2010) Vic Falls municipality dumps raw sewage into Zambezi. 12th November. [Online source: www.vicfallsbitsnblogs.blogspot.com/2016/03/vic-falls-municipality-dumps-raw-sewage.html]

Victoria Falls Bits and Blogs (August 2011) Vic Falls reports an upswing in arrivals. 31st August. [Online source: www.vicfallsbitsnblogs.blogspot.co.uk/2011/08/vic-falls-reports-upswing-in-arrivals.html]

Victoria Falls Bits and Blogs (September 2016) Vic Falls budgets $12m for water, sewer revamp. 26th September. [Online source: www.vicfallsbitsnblogs.blogspot.com/2016/09/vic-falls-budgets-12m-for-water-sewer.html]

Victoria Falls Bits and Blogs (January 2018) Victoria Falls International Airport Has the Capacity to Welcome More Airlines. 19th January. [Online source: www.vicfallsbitsnblogs.blogspot.com/2018/01/victoria-falls-international-airport.html]

Victoria Falls Bits and Blogs (July 2018) Meikles to Expand Victoria Falls Hotel. 18th July. [Online source: www.vicfallsbitsnblogs.blogspot.com/2018/07/meikles-to-expand-victoria-falls-hotel.html]

Victoria Falls Bits and Blogs (May 2019) Tourism sector targets 3 million visitors. 22nd May. [Online source: www.vicfallsbitsnblogs.blogspot.com/2019/05/tourism-sector-targets-3-million.html]

Victoria Falls Bits and Blogs (November 2019) Refurbishment works on Victoria Falls Hotel. 28th November. [Online source: www.vicfallsbitsnblogs.blogspot.com/2019/11/refurbishment-works-on-victoria-falls.html]

Victoria Falls Bits and Blogs (December 2020) Hotel slashes rates to cater for domestic market. 23rd December. [Online source: www.vicfallsbitsnblogs.blogspot.com/2020/12/hotel-slashes-rates-to-cater-for.html]

Victoria Falls Hotel (1913) Advertisement, unknown publication.

Victoria Falls Hotel (1950s) Advertisement, unknown publication.

Victoria Falls Hotel (1960s) Advertisement, unknown publication.

Victoria Falls Hotel (1970s) Advertisement, unknown publication.

Victoria Falls Hotel (1975) Advertisement, unknown publication.

Victoria Falls Hotel (July 2004) Centenary Room announced at Victoria Falls Hotel.

Victoria Falls Hotel (June 2012) Chef's Chat, Michael Ovens, Victoria Falls Hotel.

Victoria Falls Hotel (November 2012) Update on the Refurbishment of the Victoria Falls Hotel.

Victoria Falls Hotel (October 2013) Livingstone Room among world's best.

Victoria Falls Hotel (June 2015) The Stables now our exclusive Signature Wing.

Victoria Falls Hotel (July 2015) Sphinx-like, Victoria Falls sets positive future.

Victoria Falls Hotel Ltd (1914) Articles of Association. 5th January. [BRMA]

Victoria Falls Hotel Ltd (1919) Lease. 15th January. [BRMA]

Victoria Falls Hotel Ltd (1948) 34th Ordinary General Meeting. 10th February. [BRMA]

Victoria Falls Hotel Ltd (1950) 36th Ordinary General Meeting. 18th February. [BRMA]

Victoria Falls Hotel Ltd (1959) 45th Ordinary General Meeting. 20th February. [BRMA]

Viney, G. (2015) Personal communications with author, November 2015.

Viney, G. (2018) The Last Hurrah, The 1947 Royal Tour of Southern Africa and the End of Empire. Jonathan Balls Publishers, South Africa.

Walker, F. (undated) Extracts from Frederick Walker's Diary during his visit to Africa in September 1907. [CC]

Walters, P. and Fogg, J. (2007) Olive Schreiner in Rhodesia: an episode in biography. English in Africa 34: 93-109

Ward, D. (2016) Personal communications with author, April 2016.

Watt, A. (undated) History of Livingstone (unpublished document held by Livingstone Museum, c1960s).

White, B. (1973) The Trailmakers, The story of Rhodesia Railways. Supplement to Illustrated Life, Rhodesia, 31st May.

Whitehead, D. (2014) Inspired by the Zambezi, Memories of Barotseland and a Royal River - the mighty Liambai.

Williams, R. C. (1913) How I Became a Governor. John Murray, London.

Woods, J. (1960) Guide book to the Victoria Falls, S. Manning.

Zambezi Traveller (November 2013) Livingstone Room voted one of the Best in the World, eNewsletter.

Zambezi Traveller (December 2013) A key Returned. Issue 15, p.15.

Zambezi Traveller (March 2014) The Grand Lady Marks 110 Years, Issue 16, p19.

TO THE BANKS OF THE ZAMBEZI AND BEYOND

RAILWAY BUILDING FROM

THE CAPE TO THE CONGO

(1893-1910)

A detailed study of railway construction in southern Africa, focussing on the development of the line north to the Victoria Falls and beyond, hailed at the time as the southern section of the envisaged, but eventually unrealised, Cape to Cario Railway linking the length of the continent.

Fully illustrated with over 90 period photographs.

LIFE AND DEATH AT THE OLD DRIFT
VICTORIA FALLS
(1898-1905)

The Old Drift holds a pivotal place in the story of the modern development of the Victoria Falls region, marking the main crossing point on the Zambezi River above the Falls for travellers and traders heading north. Established in 1898 the crossing became the focal point for the beginnings of a small European community, before the development of the railway and opening of the Victoria Falls Bridge in 1905 shifted the focus of activity downstream.

With over 90 period photographs and fully referenced, 'Life and Death at the Old Drift' presents a detailed look at this period of great change along the banks of the Zambezi.

Sun, Steel and Spray

A History of the Victoria Falls Bridge

'Sun, Steel and Spray - A History of the Victoria Falls Bridge' presents a comprehensive look at the story of this iconic structure and engineering marvel. Built in 1904-5 as a vital link in the extension of the envisaged Cape to Cairo railway, the spanning of the Zambezi pushed engineering knowledge and construction techniques to new heights.

With over 100 period photographs and illustrations, 'Sun, Steel and Spray' is full of interesting facts, entertaining stories and information detailing the rich history of the Bridge, from conception and construction to its ongoing management and maintenance.

FOOTSTEPS THROUGH TIME

A HISTORY OF TRAVEL AND TOURISM TO THE VICTORIA FALLS

Exploring over 150 years of travel and tourism to the Victoria Falls, 'Footsteps Through Time' charts the evolution of a global tourism attraction. Discover the human heritage of this famous natural wonder and the people who have carved their names in its history - from the arrival of Dr David Livingstone in 1855, the coming of the railway and opening of the Victoria Falls Bridge fifty years later, to the development of international air travel and transformation into the modern tourism destination we know today.

Fully illustrated with over 100 contemporary images and photographs.

Printed in Great Britain
by Amazon